Life Lessons
from the Great Books
Part III

Professor J. Rufus Fears

THE TEACHING COMPANY ®

PUBLISHED BY:

THE TEACHING COMPANY
4840 Westfields Boulevard, Suite 500
Chantilly, Virginia 20151-2299
1-800-TEACH-12
Fax—703-378-3819
www.teach12.com

ISBN 1-59803-518-5

J. Rufus Fears, Ph.D.

David Ross Boyd Professor of Classics
G. T. and Libby Blankenship Chair in the History of Liberty
University of Oklahoma

Dr. J. Rufus Fears is David Ross Boyd Professor of Classics at the University of Oklahoma, where he holds the G. T. and Libby Blankenship Chair in the History of Liberty. He also currently serves as David and Ann Brown Distinguished Fellow of the Oklahoma Council of Public Affairs. Before joining the faculty at the University of Oklahoma, Professor Fears was Professor of History and Distinguished Faculty Research Lecturer at Indiana University, as well as Professor of Classical Studies and chair of the Department of Classical Studies at Boston University.

Professor Fears holds a Ph.D. from Harvard University. He has been a Danforth Fellow, a Woodrow Wilson Fellow, and a Harvard Prize Fellow. He has been a fellow of the American Academy in Rome, a Guggenheim Fellow, and twice a fellow of the Alexander von Humboldt Foundation. His research has been supported by grants from the American Philosophical Society, the National Endowment for the Humanities, the Woodrow Wilson Foundation, the Kerr Foundation, and the Zarrow Foundation.

Professor Fears is the author of more than 100 articles and reviews on ancient history, the history of liberty, and the lessons of history for our own day. Professor Fears's books and monographs include *The Cult of Virtues and Roman Imperial Ideology* and *The Theology of Victory at Rome*. He has also edited a three-volume edition of *Selected Writings of Lord Acton*. His discussions of the great books have appeared in newspapers across the country and have aired on national television and radio programs.

An acclaimed teacher and scholar who has won 25 awards for teaching excellence, Professor Fears was chosen Professor of the Year on three occasions by students at the University of Oklahoma. His other accolades include the Oklahoma Foundation for Excellence's Medal for Excellence in College and University Teaching, the University Continuing Education Association (UCEA) Great Plains Region Award for Excellence in Teaching, and the UCEA's National Award for Teaching Excellence. He was chosen as Indiana University's first-ever Distinguished Faculty Research Lecturer.

Table of Contents
Life Lessons from the Great Books
Part III

Life Lessons from the Great Books

Scope:

Great books change our lives. Great books also change *with* our lives. It is the mark of a great book that we can read it again and again and that at each stage of life, it speaks to us with a new voice. Our ever-changing life experiences allow us to see new lessons in a book that we have read and cherished long ago—or in a book that bored us in school yet fascinates us now.

In Books That Made History: Books That Can Change Your Life, we discussed 36 important works, focusing our lectures on themes of spirituality, politics, and history. This new course, *Life Lessons from the Great Books*, takes an entirely new set of writings, each of them a unique expression of the human spirit and each testimony that the list of great books is as inexhaustible as the human spirit. In our new course, we explore six themes that every one of us has experienced or will experience: the unconquerable human spirit; youth, old age, and all that is between; romance and love; adventure and courage; laughter and irony; and patriotism.

We consider each of these themes through works of literature that define our ideal of a great book. A great book possesses four qualities:

- It deals with a great theme.
- It is written in noble language.
- It speaks across the ages.
- It speaks to us as individuals.

All six themes are vast. All deal with the most central question that any individual faces: how we choose to live our lives. The unconquerable human spirit testifies that each of us does have free will. From youth through age, through all the twists and turns of life, we can make the choice to lead fulfilled lives that leave the world a better place or we can choose to make ourselves and others miserable. The twists and turns of life are frequently the result of the most powerful and irrational of motives: love. Adventure and courage call to those who see life as a challenge and choose, in the words of Theodore Roosevelt, "to go into the arena." These are the men and women of destiny, who find that one mission in life they are meant to fulfill. Laughter and irony temper our disappointments in life and allow us to enjoy our successes. Patriotism is but the enduring quality of friendship writ large. Like religion and love, patriotism can bring forth the most noble and the most base of human emotions.

Language is inherent in the enjoyment of great literature. Any language—English, Latin, Chinese, Inuit—can be noble. It is the language that elevates our spirits by its clarity, rhythm, and appropriateness. In our course, books will range from the classical purity of Cicero's Latin and the lyrical beauty of the poetry of Euripides, to the rich and supple English of Shakespeare and the German of Goethe, to the hard, clean prose of George Orwell, Elie Wiesel, and Isaac Singer.

It is the test of a great book that it speaks across the ages. The great books inform one another. As Plato drew upon Homer, Cicero drew upon both, and Thomas Moore, Erasmus, and Goethe drew upon all three. Our lectures in this course are chosen to illustrate the societies, cultures, and ideas that have shaped the great books tradition of Europe and America.

Lectures One through Six examine the lives and writings of those who have risen to the great challenges life so frequently gives each of us. Each addresses the question of why evil befalls those who are good. Such statesmen and leaders as Seneca, Boethius, and Martin Luther King, Jr., found consolation in philosophy. The Gospel of John provided inspiration for the noble Humanism of Albert Schweitzer and the profound reflections of the Russian novelist Dostoevsky. The Nobel Prize winner Elie Wiesel shatters our assumptions about the innate goodness of humans in his heart-wrenching *Night*.

In Lectures Seven through Twelve, we explore the lessons of life we can learn at each stage of our lives. We begin with the destructive adolescent love of Goethe's *The Sufferings of Young Werther* and conclude with the very different responses to old age by the Roman patriot Cicero and the Noble Prize–winning novelist Isaac Singer.

Love has been the theme of some of the greatest works of literature. Euripides captures both the life-affirming and the destructive qualities of love in his two plays *Alcestis* and *Medea*. Courtly love of the Middle Ages is illustrated in the story of Tristan and Isolde. Shakespeare, the master student of humanity, takes us from the pathos of Antony and Cleopatra to the chilling devotion of Lady Macbeth to her husband and his career, while a *Brave New World* with no room for love is pilloried by Aldous Huxley.

From Homer's *Odyssey* to Lawrence of Arabia, Lectures Nineteen through Twenty-Four let us sail and ride in search of adventure. Men and women of destiny are those blessed few who find the one mission in life that is uniquely meant for them. Adventure is the fuel for the medieval epics of *The Song of Roland* and the *Nibelungenlied* and for the exploits of modern-day and highly controversial figures, including Meriwether Lewis, William Clark, and T. E. Lawrence.

Life presents challenges, and Lectures Twenty-Five through Thirty teach us that we meet these challenges best if we remember to laugh. Great books of humor and irony make us think about important questions by teaching us that it is frequently best not to take ourselves or others too seriously. The Greeks moderated the tragedies of Sophocles with the comedies of Aristophanes and Menander. The Humanists Erasmus and More knew how to give lessons in life by playful irony. George Orwell skewered the counterfeit promises of totalitarianism with *Animal Farm*.

Like romantic love, patriotism—love of country—is one of the richest fountains of great books. The Founders of the United States cherished the ideal of patriotism and saw it exemplified in the history of Israel, Greece, and Rome. In our final six lectures, we reflect upon the meaning of true patriotism. The heroic struggle of the Jewish people for freedom was told by Josephus in his *Jewish Wars*, a work highly valued by the Founders. The ideals of the American Revolution were embodied in Joseph Addison's play *Cato*. George Washington, Theodore Roosevelt, and General George Patton exemplified those ideals. The lives and messages of these three unique Americans provide a final set of reflections on the choices each of us makes in our private, professional, and civic lives.

The enduring importance of great books is the guidance they offer in making those choices. As each of our choices must be different, so each of us will be moved by a different set of books, ideas, and historical role models. Perhaps the ultimate mark of a great book is that it leads onward to more books and to realms of ideas we never dreamed existed.

Lecture Twenty-Five
Aristophanes—Comedies

Scope:

We come now to the fifth theme in the lessons we learn from great books: laughter. Laughter, like love, is universal. One central theme of great books is how to live one's life, and laughter is fundamental to handling many of life's ups and downs. When we can no longer laugh at ourselves and our situations, then we are in dire straits. More than that, humor and irony have been instruments for profound commentaries on life and politics.

Aristophanes used comedy for the same purpose that Sophocles and Euripides used tragedy: to educate his fellow Athenian citizens for the awesome responsibility of self-government. In such comedies as *Acharnians*, *Peace*, and *Lysistrata*, Aristophanes used humor and satire to comment on the policies by which the Athenian people had begun and were conducting the Peloponnesian War, but Aristophanes was not a pacifist, and these plays were not antiwar. Far from guiding Athenian sentiment, Aristophanes reflects the mood of the Athenian people. In *Acharnians*, we find frustration at what seems to be a failed war. In *Peace*, we see the longing to end the war that led to the treaty of 421 B.C. In *Lysistrata*, we find the grim determination of the Athenian democracy in 411 B.C. to stay the course and win final victory.

Outline

I. In this lecture, we turn to a new theme: laughter and irony. Laughter and irony are natural extensions of emotions that enable us to deal with both good and bad situations in life.

II. We begin, as we always should, with the Greeks, in this case, with Aristophanes (c. 450–c. 388 B.C.).

    A. Aristophanes, an Athenian citizen, was the great comedian of the Athenian democracy.

    B. As it had been for the Athenian writers of tragedy, the war with Sparta was one of the central themes of the work of Aristophanes.

III. One of our misguided assumptions today is the idea that democracies make peaceful neighbors. History teaches us a different lesson.

    A. In 431 B.C., Pericles convinced Athens to undertake a preemptive war against the democracy of Sparta.

    B. Pericles also gave the Athenians the strategy by which they could win the war: Stay inside the walls of Athens and avoid outright confrontation with Sparta's superior infantry forces.

    C. Despite the ravages of a plague, Pericles persuaded the Athenians to continue the war.

    D. After Pericles died of the plague, a new kind of politician came to prominence in Athens—one who did not lead by moral authority but, rather, by pandering to the people. It was against these kinds of politicians that Aristophanes directed his satirical wit.

IV. Aristophanes begins *Acharnians* with a statement that he is not afraid to speak the truth. His task is to teach the Athenians that they are making a tragic mistake by continuing the war.

    A. The action begins with the hero of the play, Dicaeopolis, waiting for the assembly of the Athenians to convene.

    B. Dicaeopolis tries repeatedly to address the assembly and to protest the war but is thwarted by other important speakers.

    C. When Dicaeopolis is finally allowed to speak, he tells the chorus that the war with Sparta was actually started by Pericles to cover up the fact that his mistress, Aspasia, orchestrated a raid in Megara to capture women for her brothel.

    D. Dicaeopolis decides to make his own peace with Sparta and to begin importing embargoed goods.

    E. One by one, people approach Dicaeopolis to buy his goods, but he sells them only on the condition that his customers make peace with Sparta.

V. In the play *Peace* by Aristophanes, we learn that the god of war has stolen peace from the Earth. He has taken all of the nations of Greece, placed them in a mortar, and ground them together to continue the war.

   A. Aristophanes requested that the Athenians bring peace back to Earth, and in 421, a peace treaty was signed.

   B. By 415, however, the war had begun again. This time, the Spartans were determined to fight to the end, convinced that Athens desired tyranny over all of Greece.

VI. The last peace play by Aristophanes, *Lysistrata*, is generally seen as one more plea to end the war. The main spokesperson for peace in this play is a woman named Lysistrata.

   A. Lysistrata gathers all the women of Athens together, and they agree to forgo sexual relations with their husbands until peace is made with Sparta.

   B. The women occupy the Acropolis to seize the treasure of Athens.

   C. The men of Sparta and Athens become so desperate that they eventually sign a peace treaty.

VII. Interpreters in the 20th century have read the comedy *Lysistrata* as a plea for peace, but the Athenians of Aristophanes's time would have derived a different message.

   A. Women were constantly portrayed by Aristophanes as foolish and treacherous.

   B. By the time *Lysistrata* was produced, Aristophanes had become convinced that Athens should continue the war. To attempt another peace treaty with Sparta would be to act as foolishly as women.

   C. Aristophanes would live to see his beloved Athens defeated and dominated by the Spartans. But throughout his career, he would remain what he claimed to be: a teacher. Aristophanes taught through comedy that one should laugh despite disasters and find truth in laughter.

Suggested Reading:

Aristophanes, *The Complete Plays*.

Fears, *Famous Greeks*, Lectures Twelve through Twenty.

Hanson, *A War Like No Other*.

Questions to Consider:

1. Why can it be misleading to read Athenian comedy and tragedy through spectacles tinted with the values of the 21st century?

2. If an observer from the 46th century saw a political satire from our own day, how accurate would be that observer's assessment of the politics of America?

Lecture Twenty-Five—Transcript
Aristophanes—Comedies

In this, our 25th lecture, we continue our exploration of the life lessons that we learn from the great books, and we turn now to a new theme: laughter and irony. We've explored the themes of the unconquerable human spirit; discovered and discussed how we live our lives; we've thought about love; we've thought about adventure. But in every stage of our lives, we are in very serious trouble if we are no longer able to laugh at ourselves or find anything funny. Laughter and irony are natural human emotions that enable us to deal with the good things in life, not to take them too seriously, and not to take even the bad things too seriously.

We're going to look, in this section, at the idea of laughter in Classical Greece, and then in the age of the Renaissance—two absolutely seminal periods in human history—and end up with the 20th century. We will start with the plays of Aristophanes of classical Athens and the plays of Menander. Then, we will look at three great figures of the Renaissance: Machiavelli, Erasmus, and Sir Thomas More, each of whom used irony to point out the foibles of their own day. Finally, we will look at George Orwell's *Animal Farm*.

We begin, as we always should, with the Greeks and with Aristophanes. The Greeks invented tragedy, and also, at Athens, they invented the political satire as comedy. Both were part of your civic functions as an Athenian citizen: to watch the tragedies that were put on. The Athenians understood that you could not watch someone like Oedipus gouging his eyes out every day. That got to be too much, so you had to lighten this up, and so they put on comic performances, as well.

Aristophanes was an Athenian citizen, just as were all the writers of tragedy, and he was the great comedian of the Athenian democracy. His central theme—the decisive period in his life, as it was the decisive period in the whole history of the Athenian democracy—was the great war between the democracy of Athens and the great war with the democracy of Sparta. That war went from 431–404; it was a world war, drawing in the whole of the Greek world, as well as far off Persia, into this war and, ultimately, destroying the Athenian democracy.

You need to remember this about our Athenian democracy; it has been a leitmotif running all the way through our course: It was the first government in history based upon the ideal of the greatest good for the greatest number of citizens. It was government of the people, by the people, and for the people. It rested upon the belief that every citizen was capable of handling any governmental job, and its goal was to involve as many citizens as possible in the operation of the government. It was not a government of experts. Every decision of war and peace, of taxation, and of domestic and foreign matters was made by the entire assembly of the Athenian people coming together to vote.

Now, only males were citizens in the fullest sense of the word because, for the Athenians, the rights of citizenship—such as freedom of speech, the protection of the law—were not only rights but obligations. Only those who served in the army of Athens could be citizens, and Athens did not have a professional army, did not pay others to fight for them. Every citizen was required to be available for military service from 18 on for the rest of their lives. Old men could be brought into the military forces when circumstances required. To be a citizen, in its fullest sense, was to serve in the military.

We shouldn't be too hard on the Athenians for not allowing women to vote. Women were passive citizens; they had the protection of the law, but they weren't allowed to vote. The Athenian democracy saw no dichotomy between freedom and slavery. In fact, they defined freedom as the ability to rule over yourself and to rule over others. But another great democracy came into being in 1787, with our Constitution, in which women did not vote and in which slavery was a part of the Constitution. So let's not be too harsh on the Athenians, for their values were our values.

These values were laid out for all time in the Funeral Oration that Pericles spoke to the Athenians in the first year of this great war that had broken out in 431, the war with Sparta. [He said,] "We are a government of the people, by the people, and for the people. That is why we are a democracy. We believe in the law, both the law that was handed down to us by our forefathers and the laws that we make." Are we Americans not a government of the people, by the people, and for the people, and do we not believe in the law that was handed down to us—the Constitution—and the laws that we make ourselves?

[Pericles continued:] "We are a people who let the goods of the entire world flow into us. We believe in a free-market economy. We believe in equality of opportunity, that everyone should go as far in life as they can. We allow foreigners from all over the Greek world to come and reside here and profit. We do not think it's a shame to be poor. We do think it's a shame not to work as hard as you can to become rich. We are a tolerant society. We do not condemn you if you live a different lifestyle. We don't even give you sour looks, which might hurt your feelings. We love wisdom and beauty.

"The intellects from all over the Greek world come to us because they can flourish here amidst our freedom of thought and freedom of speech. But we are as brave as anyone else. We are patriots, and we love our country because it is worthy of loving. Taking all things together," Pericles told his fellow citizens, "we are a model to the world." It was as a model to the world in the belief that its democracy was threatened and that it was the duty of Athens to bring democracy to the entire Greek world that they had entered this war with Sparta in 431.

One of our follies of today is the idea that democracies are peaceful neighbors and that if you can just set up enough democracies around the world, there will never be another war. History teaches us very differently. The First World War was between parliamentary democracies, like Germany, Austria-Hungary—even Russia had a parliamentary democracy—and Britain, and France. What Winston Churchill pointed out is that democracies do not necessarily make for good neighbors, and when they do get into a war, they fight it through to the absolute finish. You see, in a monarchy or an empire, the king or emperor can just sit down with the other king or emperor and sign a peace treaty. The democracies rest upon the vote of the people, and once into a war, they demand that it be fought through to the finish in order to justify the losses that have been entailed. In 431, Pericles—who certainly wasn't a dictator of Athens; he was a highly regarded leader, who rested his leadership upon his moral authority—convinced Athens that they must undertake what was, in effect, a preemptive war against the democracy of Sparta. In 480, those two great democracies, Sparta and Athens, had stood side by side and defeated the Persians, who had sought to rob the Greeks of their freedom. But in the after years, they became ever more estranged from one another. Athens had its own alliance of some 243 Greek states, and Sparta had its alliance, mainly in the area of the Peloponnesian Peninsula. In 431, Pericles convinced the Athenians that Sparta was conspiring against them—Sparta intended to attack—and the great war began.

Pericles also gave the Athenians the strategy by which they would win that war. That is certainly part of a great leader, a statesman: to explain why you must go to war in a democracy and how you are going to win it. Pericles convinced the Athenians that they could not defeat the Spartans in a great single pitched battle; that their best strategy lay in coming inside the mighty walls of Athens, living inside those walls [and] using their great fleet to bring food from all over the world; and allowing the Spartans to ravage their lands. But avoid a major battle, which Sparta would win because of its superior infantry forces.

The first year came, and the Spartans ravaged the land. Then, in that first year, not long after Pericles had given his Funeral Oration celebrating the values of Athens, a plague came. For two years, this plague ravaged Athens but not Sparta. Older people looked back and said, "When this war began, Pericles ignored the warnings of the god Apollo [the god who sends plagues] that this was a holy war on the side of Sparta, that it was an unjust war by Athens, and that we would pay the price. Now we are paying it with this plague."

But despite the ravages of the plague—probably typhoid was the nature of the plague; maybe as much as 10 percent of the Athenian population died—Pericles convinced them to continue the war, pointing out now: "Maybe we never should have begun the war, but once we're in it, we must see it through to the end. We have to stay the course. If we do not, Sparta will destroy us, and all of our allies—our coalition partners—will rise up against us." Even after the death of Pericles in 429 from the plague, the Athenians stayed the course. But there rose, in the absence of Pericles, a new kind of politician, who did not lead by moral authority but by pandering to the people, professional politicians who drew heavy salaries from their public service and who followed public opinion polls. It was against these kinds of politicians that Aristophanes directed his satirical wit.

But once again, citizens are required to attend the performances of the comedy. They have a religious dimension: They are put on in honor of the god Dionysus, and an altar to the god Dionysus sits in the middle of the orchestra, where the chorus performs. You are paid a good day's wage to attend the comic performances so that you don't lose money, and it is part of your citizenship to go. But since they are not full-fledged citizens, no women attend, and that's very important in understanding the message of Aristophanes. It is only the Athenian citizens, the males. Allied members of their coalition partnership send representatives, and occasionally, other foreign states might have a representative there at this religious performance, but it is mainly the Athenian males who are watching.

In 426, Aristophanes's criticism of the chief politician Cleon—a man who had been a tanner by profession—had been so severe that Cleon was able to haul him into court, sue him, and almost ruin Aristophanes. The Athenians believed in freedom of speech, but you could also bring a libel suit against somebody—or slander suit—and take them into court.

Aristophanes starts off his play in 425—*The Acharnians*—with a little bit of a statement about [how] he's not afraid to speak the truth. His task is to be a teacher and to tell the Athenians, through this comedy, what a tragic mistake they are making by continuing the war. If any politician wants to sue him, then let it be for an Athenian jury to decide. What is more important: the politician's reputation or the truth?

The Acharnians takes its name from the chorus, and just as in Greek tragedy, [where] there is a chorus of listeners who occasionally speak in beautiful verse, giving the ordinary person's opinion about the situation, so, too, there's a chorus in comedy, giving the opinion of an ordinary Athenian about the action and issue at stake. These are the Acharnians. That's an area, a rural district of Athens, famous for its hardy farmers, who make up an important part of the Athenian army. [They are] rugged soldiers, independent and reliable the way a farmer is, taking their duties as citizens very seriously, taking the war very seriously, willing to give up their farms, allow their farms to be destroyed, in order to win this necessary and, as they see it, just war against the Spartans. They are, of course, absolutely convinced that Sparta is determined to destroy them, and they must stay the course.

The action begins with the hero of the play. His name is Dicaeopolis, and it essentially means "the good citizen." Mr. Good Citizen. He is waiting for the assembly of the Athenians to begin. The way they did that is that every citizen came into the great market area, what the Athenians called the "agora." State servants ran along with a rope that was painted red, and they began to push everybody together—gather them together—and if you came into the assembly late, you would have gotten some of the red paint on you from their circling the outer ones. That was always a reason to laugh at somebody.

Of course, the ones who always come in with the red paint are the politicians themselves. They've been dining and carousing and scheming, and so the rest of the citizens are just waiting there. Dicaeopolis stands up and says, "I want to make a speech."

The assembly says, "No, you're not on the agenda."

"Any Athenian can make a speech."

"No, you're not on the agenda for today. We are entertaining the ambassadors from the court of the king of Persia."

Indeed, since the beginning of the war, both Athens and Sparta had tried to get the king of Persia to come in as their ally, in other words, betraying the very notions of freedom which they had fought for against the Persian despotism, but now, they're trying to get the money from the Persian king. In come these delegates, and Dicaeopolis—the good citizen—asks, "Is that the same delegation we sent off years ago?"

"Yes, yes, but it has been a very hard task."

"Yeah, a very hard task to take all the gold the Persian king has given you. Look at the clothes you're wearing now. You went off in rags, and you have all these magnificent garments now, these custom-made suits. You even dress like a Persian Ah! And look how fat you've gotten."

"Well, we had to do a lot of feasting with the king of Persia and his court just to try to win them over."

"And have you won them over?"

"Not exactly, but we've brought an ambassador." The ambassador, of course—conveniently for the [Athenian] ambassadors (the delegates, the politicians that the Athenians have sent out at public cost; all of this is on the public treasury)—this ambassador who has come back from Persia doesn't speak any Greek, so they translate for him, the ambassadors do.

He says something that means something like, "The king of Persia will never give you any money in Persia."

The delegates say, "Aha! The king of Persia is willing to give us money."

Then the ambassador from Persia understands enough Greek to say, "No, no gold, *ninke poopy*."

Dicaeopolis said, "He just said it: 'No gold, *ninke poopies*.' He's calling us nincompoops!"

"No, no, no, what he said was: 'Gold coupons are coming fast.'" Immediately, they vote to extend the term of the delegates [and] send them back on this junket; that's what it is: a great political junket.

Then, Dicaeopolis tries to stand up again and speak. But no, there's another delegate who has just returned from Thrace (that's the northern part of Greece). The Athenians have been trying to lure the various tribes—less civilized tribes—of Thrace in on their side. Aristophanes's hero, Dicaeopolis, speaks out and says, "What have you been doing in Thrace? I just served a year in Thrace"—because this is a man in his 40s, Dicaeopolis, but he's in military service—"I froze up there; I was wounded up there. You, Mr. Delegate; you, Mr. Politician, you're looking very fit."

"Yes, well, we had to spend a lot of time with Sitalces, the king of the Thracians."

"And what did you do?"

"We had to drink some with him, because you know, the Thracians drink hard and …"

"Have you brought us any aid from Thrace?"

"We have; we brought these superb soldiers." They are these very old-looking men, raggedy-looking men.

"And how much have we paid for these?"

"Oh, about a million and a half for each one of them."

"That's what you've spent our money on? How much were you bribed?"

Dicaeopolis is shouted down again. This time, the politicians bring a charge against him. He is a traitor; he is attempting to delude the Athenian people. Those are very dangerous [charges]. As he's leaving the assembly, he's set upon with stones by the chorus—this is this group of old farmers from the land of Acharnia, the district of Acharnia, the Acharnians. They begin to stone him, and Dicaeopolis turns around and says, "Why are you stoning me?"

"Why, we're the men who fought at Marathon, and we fight for the democracy and freedom of Athens."

"The democracy and freedom of Athens? What you're fighting for is for politicians to get fat off of this war and for ordinary people, like you and me and our sons, to fight this war, and to suffer in it, and to die; and for women to go without husbands because they have died in this war; and children to grow up without parents, losing their father in this war, their mother dying of heartbreak. That's what you're fighting for."

"But this war is absolutely just, and we must fight it through to the end."

Dicaeopolis says, "You know, I'd like to tell you a little bit about how this war really got started." What we know about the Peloponnesian War, as this war between Athens and Sparta is called, comes to us here in the 21st century almost entirely from the historian Thucydides. He was the first truly great scientific historian. He was a contemporary of the war, and he wrote so that we might use the past to make decisions in the present and to look into the future. He was a great admirer of Pericles, and he presented the view that Pericles had of the war: that Sparta was scheming to destroy Athens, that part of Sparta's plan was to weaken the power of Athens economically. Pericles had stepped in and had the Athenians pass an embargo upon the city of Megara—Megara was part of the coalition of Sparta—in order to force Megara into the Athenian alliance and to destroy the power of Sparta. [Thucydides says,] "That's how it all got started. The Spartans were conspiring against us, and we had to take this act of embargo against Megara."

Pericles never lacked for enemies; no great statesman does. Aristophanes was one of his most bitter enemies. [In the play, Dicaeopolis] said, "Do you know how the war really got started?"

The Acharnians said, "No, tell us."

"Pericles has as his mistress, as you know, Aspasia." It's true; Pericles lived a very unconventional life. "She runs the set of brothels, correct?"

"Yes."

"She had some young men go raiding into Megara to bring back girls for her establishments."

"She did?"

"Yes, and they then raided here and carried off a couple of her girls."

"That's how it really got started?"

"Yes, and the scandal began to break, and Pericles was looking for a way to cover himself up. He said, 'Get the Athenians into a war, and they won't examine anything more closely.'"

"Wow."

"Then, you know his friend Phidias, the one who designed the whole of the Acropolis; do you know how much that cost?"

"Yes, it would cost a whole lot, but Pericles convinced us that it would be a monument for all time." And so it was.

"Yes, but we tried to look into the accounts of Pheidias, and they were all scandalously wrong, huge cost overruns. First, we prosecuted Pheidias, the architect; then, it turned out that Pericles had been in on the take, so we were coming at him from political and financial reasons. He began this war so that you would be blinded about his own personal misdeeds."

"Should we talk ill of the dead [for Pericles has been dead for four years]?"

"It doesn't matter; you need to know the truth."

"Why don't the Spartans sit down and make peace with us?"

"Because they're just as hardheaded as you are, and the two of you should sit down and negotiate and make a peace. But in the meantime, I'm making my own peace with Sparta."

So he does; Dicaeopolis makes his own peace with Sparta. He has all these goods from Sparta imported and from other parts of the world that have been embargoed and sets up his own little marketplace. Suddenly, one by one, all the visitors start coming.

"Are those eels? We haven't had smoked eels since this war began."

"Yes, yes, you can have smoked eels if you're willing to think seriously about peace."

"What about this, these little pigs? Ah, we haven't seen pigs like this since the war began."

"Uh-huh, are you willing to talk seriously about peace?"

"Yes, yes."

A bridal pair comes: "We've got no cakes for our wedding because we can't get any flour imported."

"Ah, I've got all these wonderful cakes here that have been brought in from Corinth, since I've made peace with Corinth, as well."

"Oh, our wedding would be so wonderful."

"You're going to have wedding cake, and then your husband there is going to go right off to war, isn't he?"

"Yes."

"Well, darling, why don't you go into the assembly and talk about peace?"

And so they begin to make the peace.

It turns out—in the second of his plays, Aristophanes explains to us (in his play *Peace*)—that the god of war has literally stolen peace from the Earth in order to have this bloody war. He has taken all the nations of Greece and put them into a huge mortar, with a little garlic, a little honey, a little saffron, and pounded them up just to continue this great and bloody war. "So bring peace back to Earth," Aristophanes says, and the Athenians finally do it 421. They sign a peace treaty with Sparta that is meant to last for years, and the teacher Aristophanes has had his triumph.

But it can't last. Almost immediately, the Athenians begin to ask, "Why did we go to war and fight for 10 long years just to make a peace?" By 415, the war has begun again. This time, the Spartans have become convinced that Athens is determined to be a tyrant over the entire Greek world, and this time, *they* must fight on to the end. The Athenians launch a preemptive strike against Sicily, their fleet is destroyed, and they lose thousands of young men around the walls of Sicily. By 411, their coalition partners are in revolt, the Athenians are in the most desperate economic straits [and] military straits, and this time, the Spartans are going to see it through to the end.

Then, Aristophanes produced his last peace play; it is called the *Lysistrata*. It is generally seen as one more plea for peace, one more plea to end this war. But it has changed some as the atmosphere in Athens has changed some and as Aristophanes himself has come to realize [that] once you're in a world war like this, you must fight it through to the end. The main spokesperson for peace in this play, the *Lysistrata*, is not a hardy Athenian soldier, a brave farmer; it's a woman, Lysistrata. Her name means "the dissolvers of the army."

When the play begins, it's early in the morning and Lysistrata has brought all the women of Athens together into an assembly. They vote that they will not have any relations with their husbands until the husbands agree to make a peace with Sparta. Then, Lysistrata brings the women of Sparta in, and they make the same agreement: No relations with our husbands until they bring this war to an end. The women even occupy the Acropolis of Athens to seize the treasure of Athens. The men are portrayed in very graphic form, standing outside the walls, begging their wives to come down and just have one little visit with them. One of them comes up with this little baby, and he holds it up to the walls, and says to his wife, "How could you have run off, Myrna, from our little baby?"

She talks to Lysistrata and says, "I just have to go down and see the baby a little bit." [Then to her husband:] "Oh, you haven't even changed his diaper; what is wrong with you?"

He said, "I'll change it, but couldn't we just … a little bit?" She leads him on—needs a mattress, needs some perfume—and then runs back up and leaves him there.

The men are getting desperate. Finally, the Spartans come to Athens, and the Athenians say, "Are you as desperate as we are?"

The Spartans say, "Yes, yes, we are." So they begin to make a peace treaty, but immediately, they begin to quarrel over the same reasons: "Why, we want the island of Aegina back." "We're determined to keep the Pylos." They're about to go to war again. Suddenly, the Spartans say, "Would you like to drink some?"

The Athenians say, "Yeah, let's have a little bit of wine; that will make the whole thing better." And so they begin to drink. By the time they are both good and drunk, they make a peace treaty. They march off together hand in hand, singing a Spartan war song.

Interpreters in the 20th century have taken that comedy, the *Lysistrata*, and turned it into a great plea for peace. In fact, when we were about to go to war with Iraq, the *Lysistrata* was performed all over the world as a statement of pacifism. But we must understand that each age has its own humor, and like Athens, Aristophanes had grown bitter during this war, had come to believe that Athens, indeed, had to stay the course. If we look at this play, the *Lysistrata*, with the eyes of an Athenian audience, we will see a very different meaning in it, for women were not held in high regard at Athens. Pericles completed his Funeral Oration praising Athens by simply saying, "As for the women, I suppose I'd better say a word or two. Try not to be worse than you already are, and remember that woman is best of whom the least is said." Socrates—the wisest of the Athenians—one of his most used criticisms [was:] "You are worse than a woman." Women were portrayed constantly by Aristophanes as foolish, treacherous, and lascivious.

By now, Aristophanes's message is different: "We tried peace, but it didn't work, and now, to make a peace treaty with the Spartans would be the same as to be like women, to get drunk and for the ephemeral pleasure of the moment, throw away all the glory that we have fought for. And so we must see this on through to the end." In that belief, the Athenians would reject for the next seven years every attempt by Sparta to make a peace treaty. Aristophanes would live on to see Athens absolutely defeated, its empire and navy stripped away, and his beloved Athens and its beloved democracy become dominated by the Spartans.

They stayed the course, and Aristophanes gave them the wisdom of peace early in the war [but] then followed them in their belief that the war must be won at the end. But all through, he remained just what he called himself: a teacher, teaching through comedy, teaching you to laugh despite all the disasters and to find truth in laughter.

Lecture Twenty-Six
Menander—*The Grouch*

Scope:

The Grouch conveys a simple but valuable lesson: Forgive and forget. Make the happiness of your family your supreme goal, and you will be happy. Aristophanes would have sneered at such simplicity, but homey values were just what the audience of Menander wanted to hear.

The Athenians were utterly defeated in the Peloponnesian War. They surrendered unconditionally in 404 B.C., and their political and cultural life would never be the same. The democracy continued in the 4th century, but ordinary Athenians no longer felt the deep need for involvement in political life and the willingness to sacrifice for their country that had been hallmarks of Athens in the age of Pericles. No great tragedy was written in 4th-century Athens. There was no audience for biting political satire. The public wanted the escapism of what we would today call situation comedies, and Menander supplied that desire. Menander was one of the most admired writers of antiquity; he was once asked, "Do you imitate life, or does life imitate you?" His influence can be traced from the Roman comedies of Plautus and Terence to the situation comedies of today.

Outline

I. In this lecture, we continue our focus on laughter in the exploration of life lessons from great books. One crucial lesson we have learned from such works as *Hamlet* and *The Sufferings of Young Werther* is to move on, and the first step in moving on is to laugh at oneself.

II. Menander (c. 342–c. 292 B.C.) was probably the most influential comedian ever to write. His world was 4th-century Athens, a very different place than that great warlike democracy that Aristophanes knew.

  A. The war between Athens and Sparta had destroyed Athens and much of the Greek world economically.

B. The war had brought in its wake terrible plagues and cost the lives of one out of every four Athenians of military age and one out of every two Spartans. The only losses comparable in American history took place during the Civil War.

C. After the war, both Athenians and Spartans abandoned the idea that to die for one's country is the noblest act.

D. Athens regained its empire within only a few years of its defeat by Sparta and became again a great military and economic power.

E. The new Athens employed a paid standing army and was run by professional politicians. These officials realized that the public preferred a balanced budget and tax rebates to glory.

III. The philosophy of 4th-century Athens was focused entirely on the individual. The Stoics and Epicureans emerged at this time.

    A. The Epicureans taught that the greatest evil for humans was to be involved in political life; it was the responsibility of each individual to pursue pleasure.

    B. The art of this new age celebrated the individual, not the city of Athens. Much of the art tugged at the viewers' heartstrings rather than stimulated their intellect. In his work, Menander replaced politics and satire with the comedy of ordinary, simple, human situations.

IV. Scholars had known for centuries that Menander was an influential writer, but none of his works were thought to be extant. In 1959, however, a papyrus was found containing almost an entire play by Menander, and it has enabled us to understand more clearly the brilliance of this writer. The play is called the *Dyskolos*, which might be translated as *The Grouch*.

    A. The play is set in Athens and begins with the god Pan, who describes the many festivals people enjoy at his cave. But one man, named Knemon, never enjoys himself.

    B. Knemon desires only to live by himself, shunning all social contact.

    C. Sostratos, a love-struck youth, desires to marry Knemon's daughter, but his friend attempts to dissuade him because the girl is not from a high-born family.

    D. Sostratos sends his servant Pyrrhias to speak with the girl's father, but he is chased off.

E. Sostratos, too, is also chased off by the father but encounters the girl's brother, Gorgias. Gorgias tells Sostratos that working on the family farm might help his chances of marrying the sister.

F. At this point, the action of the play is interrupted by a subplot, which seems to be common in Menander's work. A chef preparing a banquet also has an unpleasant encounter with Knemon, the grouch. Sostratos asks the chef if he can invite his beloved, along with her brother and father, to the banquet.

G. When Sostratos goes to invite the girl, he ends up rescuing Gorgias and Knemon from drowning in a well.

H. Knemon has a change of heart, endears himself once again to his family, and gives his permission for Sostratos to marry his daughter.

I. Gorgias falls in love with Sostratos's sister, and though Sostratos's father initially refuses to permit either marriage, the play ends with a joint wedding for the two young couples.

V. Menander's play influenced comedy for generations. *The Grouch* is essentially a situation comedy; its basic elements can be seen nightly on television. Just as the tragedy was the characteristic cultural statement of the Athenian democracy, the situation comedy is a characteristic cultural statement of our country and our democracy.

A. In such comedies, we learn that no problem is so serious that it cannot be solved.

B. Situation comedies can also teach good moral values.

C. In *The Grouch*, Knemon goes through a transformation that has been brought about by love. He realizes he has wasted his life and determines to make up for all the misery he has caused.

Suggested Reading:

Lape, *Reproducing Athens*.

Menander, *Plays and Fragments*.

Questions to Consider:

1. Is it fair to label situation comedies "escapist"?

2. What homey values are conveyed by situation comedies? Are all such values healthy?

Lecture Twenty-Six—Transcript
Menander—*The Grouch*

In this, our 26th lecture, we continue with our life lessons from the great books, and we continue with our focus on laughter. Laughter: It's one of the great lessons from life. I would say that there is one crucial lesson that we have learned from *Hamlet* and *The Sufferings of the Young Werther*, and that is to move on, and the first step in moving on is to laugh at yourself. Why, at the height of their troubles in the *Aeneid*—they have lost their ships; their food is all ruined— Aeneas reminds his men: "*Haec juvabit meminisse*," "Even these things will one day give us pleasure to remember."

The comic genius of Aristophanes, in his plays like the *Peace*, *The Acharnians*, and the *Lysistrata*, was a statement of the genius of the Athenian democracy. In the same way, the plays of our next great comedian, Menander, are a statement of the genius of the Athenian democracy to adapt to a new age, for as Aristophanes is the playwright and comedian of the 5th century B.C., Menander is probably the most influential comedian ever to write. His world is Athens of the 4th century B.C., and it is a very different place than that great warlike democracy that Aristophanes knew.

The war between Athens and Sparta, by its end, had destroyed Athens economically, destroyed much of the Greek world economically; it had brought in its wake terrible plagues; and it had cost the lives of 1 out of every 4 Athenians of military age and 1 out of every 2 Spartans of military age. If we compare that with the great wars of the 20th century, perhaps as many as 1 in 13 Germans died in World War II, but the cost of the great war between Athens [and Sparta] was far more terrible. The only thing comparable in our history is the American Civil War, where some states, like Mississippi, may have lost 1 out of every 4 men of military age.

In the course of that great war between Athens and Sparta, there was more than the loss of life and treasure. Something snapped in the minds of ordinary Greeks in the same way that during World War I, something snapped in the minds of ordinary Europeans : Out of that war, the Athenians and Spartans both emerged believing that nothing was ever worth that price, that it was not the noblest thing you could do to die for your country. In fact, as many who came out of the World War I generation came to believe, war is just some great farce that is pushed upon you by politicians who get into it and then cannot get out of it and, in their own self-interest, just keep it going on and on and on.

The trouble is [that] the public came to this decision, but the politicians didn't recognize it. For the next 60 years, the politicians continued—in Athens and Sparta and in other Greek cities, like Thebes and Corinth that had been equally ravaged by the war—to follow the same old policies. Athens, in fact, got back its empire; within only a few years after its defeat by Sparta, it had become a great economic power again and thought of itself even as a military power. But the Athenians were very different, and perhaps the greatest sign of this being different was the fact that this new Athenian Empire—this new Athenian democracy—did not believe in universal military service. In fact, the Athenians did not want to serve in the army at all; it was too inconvenient to their careers, cost too much time. So they had a professional standing army that they paid for. Secondly, the politicians of the day knew that what the public really wanted was not glory but a balanced budget and tax rebates.

The Athenians also came to the conclusion that they did not want to spend all that time in the assembly. Although technically all decisions were still made—as they had been a century before—by all Athenians coming into the assembly and deciding, there were [now] really professional politicians and staff members who made most of the real decisions. The Athenians were happy to leave the responsibility—the awesome responsibility—of self-government in these expert hands. The most treasured man at Athens was the head of the financial division. His task was every year not just to come up with a balanced budget but with enough money to give every Athenian a tax rebate. That's all the Athenians looked for.

It was an age in which the individual became far more important than the community. Socrates had been the most Athenian of Athenian citizens. He devoted his life to trying to make his individual citizens wiser, to understand that every decision they made in politics had moral implications, and [to remember] that Athens must base itself upon the fundamental moral principles of wisdom, justice, courage, and moderation. But the philosophy of this new age of Athens in the 4th century was focused entirely on the individual. The Stoics and the Epicureans—they came into being in Athens of the 4th century B.C. Men like Zeno taught openly, the way

Socrates had, in a covered porchway called a *stoa* (hence the name); they didn't need fancy offices. But they taught and they preached the idea that what you should achieve was absolute release from political matters. You should focus entirely on yourself. In the autonomous individual with no ties to politics lay true happiness.

The Epicureans, developed by the Athenian citizen Epicurus, taught that the greatest evil for humans was to be involved in the political life. Remember, the old Athenians of the 5th century believed—as Pericles told them—"We don't think a man who is not interested in politics is minding his own business; we think he has no business in Athens at all. If you aren't involved in politics, you aren't an Athenian citizen." But Epicurus said [politics is] the greatest evil that befalls humans. War is nothing but fantasy after a false glory, and politics is nothing but trouble. Live for pleasure. Hopefully, it will be a dignified pleasure, but even if it's just a sensual pleasure, please yourself. Pursue happiness and leave politics alone.

The art of this new age celebrated the individual, not Athens as the great city beloved of the gods. Individual portraiture began to flourish in this age. Topics that would have been thought unsuitable for the art of Phidias, the great architect and artist of Pericles, now became the most important demonstrations of art. [And] not just individual portraits but drunken old women [and] boxers. The classical art of the 5th century had been concerned with the ideal, the beautiful, and the divine; now you found much interest in a wino, drinking her flask of this wine, or a boxer whose ears were all battered, his hands all gloved, punch-drunk but going back into the ring for one more fight.

Much of the art tugged at your heartstrings rather than your intellect. A Greek work of Polyclitus in the 5th century, like the *Spear Bearer*, was meant to celebrate reason and man as a measure of all things. Now, art had a neurotic element to creep into it. The great statues of this new age, called the Hellenistic age, were [based on] themes like Laocoön, the priest of Troy who was shown in the midst of his sons being devoured by great sea serpents, and his struggling to fight them off, [with] great pathos and suffering in the face. So [there were] new themes in art, philosophy, and in comedy. Menander, citizen of Athens, [had] absolutely no interest whatsoever in politics, and every time somebody asked him, "Why don't you get involved in politics?" he said, "I am far more concerned with life." Menander took as his theme not political criticism and satire but just ordinary, simple human situations, what we almost might call—with no disrespect—the sitcom. The situation comedy is the gift of Menander in the 4th century B.C. to us today.

We had known for centuries that Menander was a very influential writer, and the Roman comedies of Plautus and Terence from the 2nd century B.C. were really little more than translations of Menander. But none of his works had actually come down to us. You must remember that in antiquity, there were no printing presses; there were no Xeroxes; there were no means of sending out thousands of emails to people. Everything had to be written by hand, laboriously, and there had to be a market to recopy it. The writing was done on papyrus, and almost none of the works of Menander had come down to us except in snippets that had been quoted.

But in 1959, there was found, under rather mysterious circumstances, a papyrus of almost an entire play by Menander, and it has enabled us to understand far more clearly the brilliance of this writer. It is called the *Dyskolos*; we might translate it as *The Old Grouch*, or *The Misanthrope*. The play is set in Athens, and it begins with the god Pan, the god of enjoyment and the god of rural festivals. He's standing in front of a cave, and he says, "Here we are. We're in Acharnia again," just where the old farmers of the *Acharnians* [were] from. [Pan says:] "It's a rural land, you know, and hard on the back, hard to scratch a living out of this rugged land, but people farm it. Then they come here to my cave to worship me, so I get a lot of traffic out here, people from the city of Athens coming out here to have festivals, enjoy themselves. But I will tell you one old man who never enjoys himself, and that's that man right there: Knemon. He hates everybody. Why, he has only one desire in life: to see nobody. Oh, he had a wife at one point, and they even had a child; she had been married before and he had a stepson with her, and then they had a daughter.

"She divorced him; she just could not stand him any more, constantly complaining about everything. The son is a good, fine young fellow; you can't imagine how he would come from a father like that and even be raised by him a little bit. But he takes care of his mom. The dad lives off by himself with just his daughter, and she is the only one that he will talk to. He has a servant—an old lady—but he yells at her all the time and she yells back at him, so there they live on this little farm. See that young fellow there? That's Sostratos. He has come out from the city—you can tell by his clothes—and let me say [that] he's love struck. Take it from there, Sostratos."

The play begins. There's Sostratos; he's a boy in his early 20s, very fancily dressed, very white complexion—he has never been out in the Sun at all—with soft hands. He is standing there, just cow-eyed, in love. He's standing there and standing there and can't even move, and his friend, who is far more cynical—a young man, too, but far more cynical—comes up and says, "What's up, old pal?"

"I'm in love."

"You're in love?"

"Yes, I'm in love."

"But who with?"

"Do you see her over there?"

"Who? That country girl picking up the jug of water out of the well; that's who you're in love with? I'll admit she's pretty, but there are all the girls in town. I thought you had a girlfriend every day."

"I used to before I saw her. I came out here to help my mom prepare a festival to Pan, and just by chance, I saw this girl and was struck by a thunderbolt of love for her."

"I don't know; that sounds serious, but I think I can help you."

"Would you?"

"Yes, you want to get her in bed; is that right?"

"Only after I marry her."

"Oh, now, that's a problem. Oh, no, if you just wanted to sleep with her, I think I can work that out probably; I'm very cagey. But marriage, that's a different business, and I'm not going to help you with that, old pal. First of all, she doesn't have any money. Now you know when you get married, your father is going to want you to marry a girl from a high-born family that brings a big dowry into the wedding. He's not going to let you get married [to a poor girl]. He'll probably cut you off, renounce you, if you marry a poor girl. Secondly, a girl like that is so innocent and sweet, you're not going to be happy with her."

"I want to marry her."

"I'm going to try to help you, but I don't know what to do. Have you taken these steps so far?"

"Yes, yes, I've sent my servant."

"Not Pyrrhias, that little fool; you sent him? What did he do?"

"I sent him over to the old man—the father of this girl—to see if I could call upon her."

"Oh, that's going to end in disaster."

Sure enough, the next scene is of Pyrrhias running onto the stage— the servant—and the old man is chasing him. "I'm going to kill you!"

He's throwing these clods of dirt and rocks after him and chasing him for almost a mile. Finally, the old man stops and turns to the audience and says, "Do you know who I most admire in the world? Perseus, that figure from mythology. First of all, he had a horse with wings on it, and he could fly away and leave the whole world behind. Then, he had a Gorgon, the head of it, and he could show that to people and they turned to stone. I'd turn the whole world into stone and I'd fly way away. How much I hate people. They are nothing but the biggest pest in the world. Now I have moved out here so I didn't have to fool with my wife and that foolish son. I've got my little girl here, and that's all I need. I farm my land. Yeah, I've got a little money put aside, but I never spend it, and I don't invite anybody out here to do work for me. I can't stand talking to them. I'd rather break my back than have to say hello to anybody. I just want to be left alone. Here comes this guy knocking on my door, wanting to talk with me about something. If you come back, I'll kill you."

Sostratos says, "What did you do, servant Pyrrhias, how did you make such a mistake?"

The servant says, "I didn't do anything. I just knocked on his door."

"No, you did more than that; you said something to irritate him."

"No, that man was born irritable. I said nothing to him, and he took off after me like that. I'm not going back there. You find somebody else to talk to him. Or better yet, just give up this idea of dating this girl."

"I don't know what to do. Let's go up there and talk a little bit." Sostratos walks up there and [says], "Maybe I can talk to the old man myself."

His friend says, "This is a very bad idea." He goes up there, and he's standing around in the forecourt of the house.

The old man comes out again. "What are you doing here? Don't you see this is private property? Don't you see that sign up there? 'No trespassing; reserve the right to kill anyone who steps on my property'? What are you doing standing here?"

"I'm waiting for a friend."

"You're waiting for a friend? Oh, well, let me go get you a bench. Let me put a bench out here for you. Can I get you some wine maybe? I mean the whole world ought to be able to just come here like a public park. You get out of here." He takes a hoe after him, chases him away. "There, now I'm finally going to have a little quiet and calm."

Here's poor Sostratos, still standing afar, trying to see the girl come out of the house, so he can just catch a glimpse of this girl he was falling so much in love with. Then suddenly, a young man walks up to him, nice-looking man but dressed in very country clothes, very sunburned, very calloused hands, and it is, in fact, the brother of this girl that he is in love with, her brother Gorgias. Gorgias comes up and says, "Excuse me, sir, I've noticed you standing around here all morning. May I ask what you're doing?"

"Ah, well, I'm trying to have a conversation with that girl."

"That girl up there?"

"Yes."

"Why would you like to talk to her, sir?"

"She's so beautiful."

"Now let me tell you something, buddy," says the brother. "I know about fine-dressed young men like you. You've come out here trying to have a dalliance with my sister, haven't you?"

"Oh, you're her brother."

"Yes, I'm her brother, and I'm going to break your neck if you don't get out of here right away, and if I ever catch you around here, I'm going to break your neck."

"This is the most unfriendly family I've ever seen. How can such a sweet girl have this terrible father and this terrible brother?"

"I told you, get out of here."

"I'm going to appeal to you, sir."

"What?"

"I have only the most honorable intentions toward your sister."

"You do?"

"Yes, I want to marry her."

"You want to marry her, a rich fellow like you?"

"Yes, I wouldn't ask for a dowry or anything. I just want to meet her and talk to her. If she's as sweet as she looks, I'll give her my heart forever."

"I believe you're telling the truth, but it's impossible. Go find another girl to love. My father will never let her go. He's deeply jealous of her; she's the only person in the world he talks to. He hates everybody else. In fact, he told me once, 'I'll only marry my daughter to somebody just as mean as I am.' You'll never find anybody like that. So it's a hopeless task."

"Isn't there any way I could win him over?"

"Oh, I don't know. I'll tell you what. If you come and work the farm with me, maybe he'll take you seriously. Have you ever done any real hard work?"

"No."

"Let me see your hands."

"You'll get blisters immediately. We'll get you some gloves, get you some work clothes. Here, take this pick and go out and help me dig some ditches."

"All right."

They labor all day long. Poor old Sostratos, by the end of the day, his back is almost broken. He's bent all over and can barely walk; his hands are bleeding; his feet are all torn from the cactus plants out where they had been digging around in the rocks and the stones. But he gets his little bit of reward, because the girl gives him a drink from the well. The water is the sweetest he has ever tasted, and she is just as sweet as she looks, and she's taken with him. She gives him a lovely smile, and the brother says, "I think this would be a fine man for you to get to know." She's much taken with him. Suddenly, the old man comes out again. He starts throwing rocks again, and then he throws them at his stepson as well and says, "I told you to stay away from here; you bring nothing but trouble. [And] tell your mom to stay away from here. Get back in the house, girl."

At this point, the action is interrupted by a subplot; these plays of Menander always have a subplot. This subplot is of a festival—a great banquet and religious festival—that's going to be conducted out there in the cave of the god Pan. In fact, who's going to be conducting it is the mother of Sostratos. The first step is when the caterer comes out. He's a very, very serious character. He's a chef, and he takes his work very seriously, and he has thousands of customers in Athens. This is one of his big customers, the mother of Sostratos. He's going to lay on a great festival—the servant is dragging along the sheep that they are going to sacrifice; all kinds of sweet cakes and wonderful stews are going to be prepared out there—and have a great country banquet.

But he realizes when he gets out there that he has not brought with him a kettle. He goes back, knocks on the door of old Knemon—who is the neighbor—and says, "May I have a kettle?" Knemon brings out, of course, a kettle, and tries to bash him in the head. He runs away, but he keeps on with his work there, and says, "I'll just roast the sheep whole; I guess that's what I'll have to do. That is the meanest man I ever saw, as well."

Sostratos keeps hanging around, comes to where the festival is going to be, and says, "Could I invite some other people; could I invite this girl I'm in love with and her brother? Maybe we could even invite her father."

One of the servants, of course, is worried that he is not going to have enough to eat. But the chef says, "All right, go ahead and invite them."

Sostratos starts going back to the house of old Knemon when suddenly, there is all this shrieking. It is the servant of Knemon, this old lady who works there and takes care of this grumpy old man—this old grouch—and she is shrieking, "The master has fallen into the well. I dropped the bucket today. He won't ever buy a good rope, so I dropped the bucket; it fell down into the well. Then he said, 'I'm going to take you and drop you down into the well.' He tried to tie me to a little rope to ease me down in. But I escaped away and he said, 'I can't stand it anymore,' so he lowered himself down into the well to get the bucket; that's how cheap he is. But the rope was no good; it has broken, and now he's drowning. He's drowning!"

Sostratos runs, along with the brother, Gorgias, and they run up to the well. The brother—the old man's stepson—lowers himself down into the well and tries to save this father who has been so mean to him. He says, "I can't. We're both going to drown."

So brave Sostratos goes down into the well, and the two of them grapple and pull, and grapple and pull, and finally, save the old man and pull him out of the well. When the old man comes to, he turns to his son and says, "You risked your life to save me. I've been so mean to you all these years. If anybody had been as mean to me as I was to you, I would have said, 'Just drown.' You're a fine young man, and I've denied it all these years. And your mother; how is she? Have her come; go get her right now. I want to make up for all the years of sadness that we have had. I want us all to get back together."

"Dad, while you're feeling so kind, see this young man here?"

"Yes, he helped save me, too. What a fine young man you were. I wish I could do just something for you. So brave you were, coming down to get me like that."

"Dad, you can do something for him."

"What?"

"Let him marry your daughter."

"Oh, it would be the chief delight of my life to think she was married to such a fine young person. And as I say, I've got a little bit set aside. I'll make you a rich dowry."

"I don't want a dowry, sir. I'm wealthy myself and I just want to be with your daughter forever."

"Oh, can things ever be finer than this?"

"Yes, Dad, they could be a little bit finer."

"What is that?"

"Sostratos, your new son-in-law to be …"

"Yes?"

"He has a beautiful sister."

"He does?"

"Yes, and I've fallen in love with her, just this afternoon."

"Oh, well, marry her with all my blessings."

"Now wait a minute," the boy's dad comes in. Sostratos's dad comes in; this is a wealthy man. He says, "Wait a minute; it's bad enough you've got to have this penniless bride, but no, I'm not giving my daughter in marriage to somebody who doesn't have any money."

Sostratos says to his wealthy father, "Dad, what are you saving all that money for? Don't you know that you can t take it with you?"

"I want to leave it to you."

"Dad, I can live on love and so can my friend here. Let's have a joint wedding."

"All right, let's do."

That is how the play ends, with this lovely marriage.

This play from Menander would influence comedy generation after generation. The comedies of Aristophanes, with their deep, biting political satire, were too difficult to interpret—[with] all the contemporary references—and moreover, just not interesting. But this [work of] Menander is a play about life. In fact, that was the tribute made to Menander: "Oh, Menander, do you imitate life or does life imitate you?" What is this play of Menander, *The Old Grouch*, except a situation comedy, a situation comedy about nothing? Every element in this situation comedy of Menander can be seen every night on TV all over our country and, indeed, all over the world. In fact, as the tragedy—*Oedipus the King*, *Ajax*, or *Medea*— was the characteristic cultural statement of the Athenian democracy in its great day, so the situation comedy is a characteristic cultural statement of our country today and of our democracy.

The running servant who rushes onto the stage and rushes off and carries much of the action—who is that but Cosmo Kramer on the old series *Seinfeld*? How did *Seinfeld* bill itself? A show about nothing. Now tragedy [and] even the comedies of Aristophanes are deeply about politics, but *Seinfeld* and every situation comedy that comes on is about affairs of nothing. Instead of somebody gouging their eyes out in pursuit of wisdom, like in *Oedipus*, you have someone who falls in love at the beginning of the show and it's resolved by the end of the show. No problem is too serious that it cannot be resolved. Then, the characters in these situation comedies of Menander, what gives them such a sense of awakening our admiration is they have no responsibilities whatsoever, the same way that in *Seinfeld*, they feel no responsibility whatsoever for their various actions and the consequences that come about as a result.

Now, situation comedies are very good, and they can touch our heartstrings in very special ways. They can teach very good moral values, and there is no better way—I think—of reaching children, if they can relate to it, than an old situation comedy like *Leave It to Beaver*. That, too, is simple. The situations are all resolved in very short order, but it teaches good values. Hardly anything that Beaver does doesn't end up with a good lesson: love of father, love of mother, and the fact that parents are willing to sacrifice to help you.

Let's think about our Menander in [terms of] the life lesson. First of all, here's a man so angry at the world—as some of us can get, thinking the world has nothing but bad in it—that he has made his life miserable, made his wife's life miserable, [is] trying to make his son's life miserable, and trying to make his daughter's life miserable, holding onto a little piece of land and a little bit of money. Then, there comes in this young man, motivated by one of the noblest of all emotions, just love, and that is all he wants: pure love with this lovely girl. Love, then, becomes the key that offers a solution. Then, when the old man has fallen into the well, his son puts aside all the wrong his dad has done to him, puts aside the fact that he could also inherit the farm right then and there, goes down into the well, and aided by this young man who's in love, brings him up.

The father goes through a transformation. He realizes his whole life has been wasted, and he decides—just as I keep reminding you to do—"I'm going to move on, and from this moment onward, I'm going to see the fun in life. I'm going to let my children enjoy themselves. I'm going to let them take care of me, and I am going to try to be a friend and neighbor to the whole world. I may be old, but I can still make up for all the misery that I have caused."

So the transformation of the old grouch into a nice old chap: not a bad way to spend the afternoon in Athens, watching the [play of] Menander.

Lecture Twenty-Seven
Machiavelli—*La Mandragola*

Scope:

The comedy *La Mandragola* conveys an unpleasant truth: When we are seduced and betrayed, it is generally because we have seduced and betrayed ourselves.

Niccolò Machiavelli is widely known as the author of *The Prince*, one of the most influential and controversial treatises on politics ever published. Less well known is the fact that he is also the author of perhaps the finest comedy in the Italian language, *La Mandragola*. In Machiavelli's day, a potion from the mandrake root (*la mandragola*) was thought to enhance sexual potency for men. Machiavelli's comedy brings together two plots. One is the desire of a young, rakish nobleman of Florence to seduce a beautiful married woman. The other is the desire of that married woman, Madonna Lucrezia, and her doltish attorney husband to conceive a child. Medical science and the church come together in this play with posturing, posing, and deception to fulfill everyone's desires. The play ends with all the characters happy in their self-deceit.

La Mandragola is funny. It is written in crisp, clear Italian. It speaks across the ages in the sense that its theme is echoed routinely in the situation comedies of today. But above all, *La Mandragola* offers insight into the less-than-salubrious moral character of Machiavelli.

Outline

I.   In this lecture, we look at what has been considered the greatest comedy ever written in the Italian language: *La Mandragola* (*The Mandrake*) by Niccolò Machiavelli (1469–1527). In many ways, the play reminds us of *The Grouch* by Menander, who was influential in the age of the Renaissance. Machiavelli would have known Menander through the plays of Terence and Plautus.

II. Machiavelli was the very essence of a Renaissance man.

    A. Machiavelli was born in the creative center of the Renaissance: Florence.

B. He wrote and spoke Latin fluently, and though he always longed for political power, he played his role largely behind the scenes.

C. Florence was a republic and was torn by partisan politics. Machiavelli made his way through the partisan strife, winning the trust of the council that governed the Republic of Florence.

D. He was sent on expeditions abroad and spent some time at the court of the pope.

E. In 1512, the Medici family came back into power, and Machiavelli was banished from Florence.

F. Machiavelli wrote *The Prince* while in exile, and though he hoped the work would win him the favor of the Medicis, it failed in that regard, and he never regained his earlier influence.

III. Machiavelli supported himself in part by writing plays. Italy was absolutely enraptured by his comedy *La Mandragola*.

A. *La Mandragola* was written in Italian and set in Florence.

B. The play begins with its hero, Callimaco, telling his servant Siro that he has fallen in love with Madonna Lucrezia, who is married.

C. Callimaco consults with his friend Ligurio to devise a way for Callimaco to sleep with Lucrezia.

D. Ligurio decides that Callimaco should tell Nicia—Lucrezia's husband—that he is a distinguished medical doctor and that he can provide a cure for the couple's infertility.

E. Callimaco, disguised as a doctor, tells Nicia that the infertility can be cured if Lucrezia drinks a potion made of mandrake root. However, Nicia must find someone else to sleep with his wife because the first to do so after she drinks the potion will die.

F. Callimaco, Nicia, and Ligurio go to church and bribe Friar Timoteo to persuade Lucrezia to go along with the plan.

G. After Lucrezia agrees, Nicia captures Callimaco (who is disguised as a drunken student), takes him home, and the task is done.

H. Callimaco explains to Lucrezia who he really is, and she welcomes his embrace. She is so taken with him that she convinces her husband to give Callimaco a key to the house so that he can come by whenever he wants.

IV. Given the definition we have already established, can we say that *La Mandragola* is a great book? The language of Machiavelli is beautiful, and the theme of the play, while not noble, certainly speaks across the ages. But can a person with an evil mind write a truly great book?

   A. We come back to the ideas Machiavelli espoused in *The Prince*: There is no right and no wrong and all that matters is expediency and success.

   B. One of our life lessons may be that evil sometimes wins out in the end and that even those who seem good and virtuous will perform evil, destructive deeds if it is convenient and expedient for them to do so.

Suggested Reading:

Burckhardt, *The Civilization of the Renaissance in Italy*.

Fears, *Books That Have Made History: Books That Can Change Your Life*, Lecture Twenty-Four.

Machiavelli, *The Comedies of Machiavelli*.

Questions to Consider:

1. Is *La Mandragola* a play about deception or self-deception?
2. Can a morally bad person write a great book?

Lecture Twenty-Seven—Transcript
Machiavelli—*La Mandragola*

In this, our 27th lecture, we continue our exploration of the life lessons that we gain from the great books and continue with our theme of irony and laughter. We look at what has generally been considered to be the greatest comedy ever written in the Italian language, *The Mandrake* (*La Mandragola*) by Niccolò Machiavelli.

We've looked at Aristophanes and Menander. The poetry and beauty of Aristophanes's comedies were very much directed at his own day. Menander, by contrast, as we have seen, spoke to worlds that came afterwards. The Romans had little interest in the politics of Athens in the 5th century B.C., but they found the plays of Menander to be wonderfully escapist. Plautus and Terence, in the 2nd century B.C., translated Menander, and through them, Menander influenced the later Roman Empire, influenced the Middle Ages, and continued to be a very important literary figure and influence on the age of the Renaissance. Machiavelli himself was much devoted to the plays of Terence and Plautus and, through them, to Menander himself, and that view—do you imitate life or does life imitate you?—is Menander.

The Renaissance is a period that I believe begins in the late 14th century. We defined the Middle Ages—our age of courtly love and chivalry in the stories of *The Song of Roland*—as extending from 312, the conversion of the Emperor Constantine to Christianity, and going right on up until 1453 and the fall of that city of Constantinople. But already a century before, new stirrings had begun, above all, in Italy. Dante is still a figure of the Middle Ages—in many ways, the summation of the Middle Ages—but the poet Petrarch, who died in 1374, is utterly absorbed by the attempt to re-create—give a rebirth to—the world of classical antiquity. That is what *renaissance* means: "[the rebirth of] the world of classical antiquity." It was an age of new understanding of the Greek language; it was an age of exploration. In 1492, Columbus, a true figure of the Renaissance, comes to what he saw as a new world. New trade routes [are] being developed, [along with] new forms of political entities: The nation-state in France, Spain, and Britain is coming into being.

Niccolò Machiavelli was the very essence of a Renaissance man. He was born in 1469 in the creative center of the Renaissance—

Florence—which saw itself as a new form of the ancient city-state, with its democratic politics, professional army, magnificent culture, and figures like Michelangelo. Machiavelli was born to sort of a modestly well-off man at a small estate who saw to it that Machiavelli got the most contemporary kind of education. Above all, it was an education in these very classic books that we've been talking about.

Machiavelli wrote Latin very fluently [and] could speak it very fluently. It was, after all, the language if you wanted to be a diplomat; it was the language if you wanted to be a lawyer; if you wanted to be a doctor. Machiavelli fell in love with the classics. He knew some Greek, but he basically drew upon the Latin classics and then translations in Latin from the Greek classics. He got into the world of bureaucratic administration. He always longed for power, but instead, he played a role behind the scenes.

Florence was a republic. It had driven out the old royal family and dictatorship of the Medici family, and it was now a republic, literally torn by partisan politics. Machiavelli made his way delicately through the partisan strife of his day, winning the trust and confidence of the council that governed the Republic of Florence. He was sent on expeditions to France, Germany, and to other Italian states. He spent some time at the court of the pope, who was, in that period, a great temporal power in himself. He began to draw the lessons of what made a successful statesman.

But in 1512, the Medici family came back into power. The republic fell, and all those who had been closely associated with the republic found themselves now listed as traitors, and one of these was Machiavelli. He was briefly imprisoned and tortured, said to have been engaged in a conspiracy to assassinate the Medici ruler. [Although] he was found guilty, his death sentence was commuted, but he was forbidden to enter the city of Florence upon pain of death.

Here he was in middle age, having fallen from the power he thought he had, a failure. He settled in his old father's estate and began to reflect upon what had happened to him. Out of that misery, he brought forth one of the most influential political books ever written, *The Prince*. Writing it at a white heat in 1513, he distilled all of his knowledge of classical antiquity about why leaders are successful and drew the principle that what is important is to get and keep power. Morality plays no role whatsoever in the successful leader. In fact, the successful leader must be able to lie, steal, and kill. He must be cruel and stingy and utterly treacherous, all the while, however, presenting a face of benevolence to the world. He must be feared rather than loved; better to be hated than loved because people will do things for you out of hate when they will not do them out of love because they fear you. The worst thing you can do is to be seen to be weak. Christianity matters not at all, although the good ruler will adopt the maxims of Christianity and seem to be very pious.

The book was thought to be so scandalous—and so true—that it had the absolute opposite effect that Machiavelli had wanted. Machiavelli hoped that the Medici ruler would read it—Lorenzo de' Medici—[and] be so taken with the brilliance of Machiavelli that he would invite him back, and Machiavelli would have his old job and more back. Lorenzo de' Medici and those who read [the book] said, "It's absolutely true, but we can't [let it] seem [that we] agree with it," so Machiavelli never got back into the power that he wanted.

But one way he supported himself was by writing plays, and Medici finally would give some honors and awards to Machiavelli, not for *The Prince* that we associate him with (*The Leader* or *Il Principe*), but for his comedies. Above all, Italy was absolutely enraptured by Machiavelli's play—his comedy—*La Mandragola* (*The Mandrake*), which seems to have been produced probably around 1516 or 1517, maybe 10 years before Machiavelli's death in 1527. [It] continued to be revived and produced again and again, sometimes presented before the Renaissance courts of Italy, including the Medici court, and gained a good deal of money and a good deal of fame for Machiavelli.

The Mandragola: The word comes from the root called a "mandrake," which from its very shape was believed in the Middle Ages and Renaissance to bring about male potency. Some of the sitcoms that we were talking about in our last lecture might very well be sponsored by our modern equivalent of the mandrake, and that's what this was, *La Mandragola*. The play is set in Florence, but it is very carefully adapted from characters that we would have found in Menander. In fact, Machiavelli actually translated one of the plays of Terence called "The Woman of Andros," and in this case, his actors have Greek-like names for the most part, there in *The Mandrake*.

It begins in Florence, it has a lovely poetic prelude, and Machiavelli writes it, of course, in Italian. Machiavelli was the founder, in many ways, of the modern Italian language. It was expected when he wrote *The Prince* that he would write it in Latin; that was the language of educated communication. But instead, he created a vigorous, strong, clear Italian prose, and the prose of *The Mandragola* is an absolute joy to read: short sentences, lots of witticism, beautiful Italian.

The Mandragola is written in Italian, set in Florence, and it begins with the hero (let's call him, if this is what he is) of the play, Messer Callimaco. Callimachus [is] a Greek name; he's a figure from Menander. Messer Callimaco is discussing his very desperate situation with his servant Siro.

The servant says, "I'm always willing to listen to your troubles, master."

Callimaco says, "I know, but I've poured my heart out to you so many times, you must be exhausted by now."

"No, no, no, I'm delighted to hear more."

"It's like this: I am so in love with Madonna Lucrezia."

"Tell me again how that came about."

"You know, for many years, I lived in France."

"Yes, I was there with you."

"When I was 10 years old, my family sent me to France to be educated, and for 10 years, I studied. I learned Latin very, very well; I learned about the law. I was going to come back to Florence and start up a career, but all the wars broke out in Italy—the invasion of the French king—so I just stayed there for 10 more years. But finally, I had to come back.

"I had decided to live permanently in Paris, but one day, I was entertaining, as I always did—because I'm wealthy and well-born—an Italian nobleman, Messer Calfucci. He had come from Florence, and I had invited a number of French aristocrats over to meet with him. They got into an argument that almost led to a duel over whether Italian or French women are the more beautiful. They debated this back and forth, and it got more and more violent, until finally, Messer Calfucci said he would challenge any Frenchman to show a woman as beautiful and as virtuous as Madonna Lucrezia, his in-law. He described her beauty, and he described how virtuous she was, and just from that very description, I fell in love with her. I had to come back. So I came back to Florence just to catch a glimpse of this wonderful, beautiful woman. I looked at her, and just having seen her from afar, I realized everything he had said was true."

Just like our Sostratos, he has been captivated by the thunderbolt that is love from afar.

"I fell absolutely in love with her. Now the question is: How can I sleep with her?"

"Yes, because I was going to say, master, she's already married."

"I know she is, to Messer Nicia." (Nicia is another Greek name, Messer Nicia.) "Yes, I know she's married to him, and there's no chance of a divorce, of course, but I just want to sleep with her."

"I don't know; that's going to be hard to do because she is—as they say—very, very virtuous. Have you taken any steps about it, master?"

See how we're following the plot of *The Old Grouch*?

"I have; do you know Ligurio?" That's an Italian name, and this was in the day before ethnic stereotypes. The Florentines were convinced that the people of Genoa—Liguria—were very scheming, treacherous, and stingy; so Ligurio was the Ligurian. The meaning aroused a little snicker in the Florentine audience.

"Yes, I've talked to Ligurio, that moocher, that sponger; he's a parasite. All he does is hang around looking for free meals."

"I know, but I don't mind giving him free meals because he's very clever, very clever indeed. He has been thinking about how to get this done."

"I think you're in desperate straits, master, if you are trying to work through that Ligurio, but I wish you all the best."

"Stay tuned, because I may need you again."

Ligurio comes in and says, "I've been looking into this, and it's going to be difficult."

"Why? Why is it going to be difficult for me to get to sleep with Madonna Lucrezia?"

"Step one: She is married. Step two: She is very chaste and virtuous. Step three: Her husband keeps a very close eye on her. However, they have been married six years and still do not have a child, and they desperately want a child. That's step one. Step two: Although he's a very good lawyer, her husband is the stupidest man in all of Florence; he's a real fool. Thirdly: The mother of Lucrezia, Sostrata"—another Greek name—"is desperate to have a grandchild, as well. I think she's a real woman of the world, and she might help us carry this all off."

"All right, what's our next step?"

"I have talked to Messer Nicia. I get free lunches from him, too, and he has taken me into his confidence about how much he wants to have a child. He tells me that the doctors have advised him to take his wife to the baths, to the spa, and there, they can relax, drink some water [sulfur water], and he thinks that might be the cure for this infertility. I don't know; I worry about that."

"I do, too, Ligurio, because what other boys might she meet there at that baths? No, I think we've got to come up with a scheme that will enable us to carry it out here in Florence."

They begin to plot.

"You speak Latin, don't you, pretty well, Messer Callimaco?"

"Yes, I speak Latin quite well."

"Can you mumble a few things about medicine?"

"Oh yes, yes, that's part of our liberal arts curriculum. We learned a little bit about medicine."

"All right. Messer Nicia speaks Latin, and he thinks that anybody who speaks Latin must be honest; that's what a fool he is. So we will claim maybe that you are a medical doctor and that I've heard you have come from France, that you are the most distinguished medical doctor of your day, and that, in fact, your specialty is infertility."

"Oh, I'm liking this."

"Yes, you leave it all to me, your good friend Ligurio"—the plot is now thickening—"and we'll work this out. What we've got on our side is the fact that all people are really evil, and you just gotta find the right key to turn that evil dimension in anybody, even a lady as chaste as Madam Lucrezia, even that lady. You'll see; we'll work it out."

Ligurio goes back to the husband of Lucrezia—Messer Nicia—and talks to him, and says, "I cherish your friendship so much, and I cherish so much the confidence that you've shown in me that I think I have gotten a handle on this question."

"What is it?"

"I have met, made the acquaintance of, the most distinguished doctor in France."

"Oh, I told you; I don't want to go all the way to Paris or somewhere like that."

"No, he's visiting here in Italy. He's visiting right here in Florence, and I think we should go and get an infertility cure from him."

"I'm afraid he'll get us started in this and then drop us."

"No, no, no, I've talked to him, and the case interests him."

"Really?"

"Yes, the case interests him, and he will see it through to the conclusion. Just go and meet him."

They go and knock on the door, and Callimaco, dressed as a doctor, comes out: "*Bona dies, magister domine.*"

"*Vobis bona dies, magister doctor.* You speak Latin beautifully."

"Yes, yes, I do. What is the trouble here? Should we speak in Latin or in Italian?"

"Let's speak in Italian so that I—Ligurio—can understand what's going on, if that will be all right."

"Yes."

"The difficulty is this: My wife has been unable to have a child."

"Of course, the first problem might be you."

"No, no, no, I may be old, but I know that is not the problem; I'm telling you that right now."

"All right, then, that just was the first possibility. I just had to ask that. Then, secondly, it must lie with her." Then he quotes some Latin about the causes of female infertility and says, "I think what we need to do is to allow me to develop a potion for you out of the mandrake. We will give it to your wife, we will mix it up, and I'm the only one who actually has the formula. I will just tell you this: It is recommended by the king of France himself. There would be no heirs to the throne of France right now if I had not intervened for the queen."

"Really?"

"Yes. Oh, and how many noblemen of France now have heirs, male children, because it always almost brings forth a male child."

"A male child? This is even better."

"Oh, I know. So it will work."

"I'm ready for it then. You are so kind. Will it cost?"

"No, I tell you what: I'm interested in your case; I will cut my fees."

"This is better and better, because I'm real stingy."

"However, there is a side effect." (Like the little side effects in the commercials today; when you listen to them, they are much worse than what they are curing.) "There is a side effect."

"What is that?"

"After she takes it, the first man to have relations with her will die."

"What?"

"Yes."

"I'm not going to do that!"

"I'm just telling you that is a side effect. Unless you can find somebody to sleep with your wife, you'll die."

"Well, no; Ligurio you've gotten me into the worst possible situation."

"Now, wait a minute Messer Nicia; let's just ponder this a little bit. Do you really want a child?"

"Yes."

"Doesn't God want you to have a child?"

"Well, maybe."

"Wouldn't God be willing to forgive this in order to have another person to worship him?"

"Yes, but somebody might die. Doctor, explain to him."

"Yes, well they might die, but you know, it may be one in four lives."

"Oh, well, that's not too bad of odds. But there is a problem," Messer Nicia says. "My wife is beautiful and absolutely virtuous. She would never agree to this."

"Oh, maybe we can work our wiles there, too, if you're really serious about going ahead with this."

"I am serious. I will do anything to have a child."

Off they go, and of course, where [do] they go to convince Lucrezia, the wife, to have this illicit affair? All this is just Machiavelli talking. I'm just giving you an influential comedy; you cannot blame me. It's no more ribald than some of Shakespeare's plays and very tame [compared] to what you would see on TV today; isn't that correct? Yes, so just listen on. [They go] to the local friar. One of Machiavelli's pet hatreds is the church and all the hypocrisy of the church. [Consider] the fact that Jesus said the way to the kingdom of God is to sell all you have and give it to the poor, and then look at the church and all its wealth. [Machiavelli] believes that most friars and most priests are just frogs who have gone into this line of work because they don't have to do any real work, and they are all greedy and malevolent.

This is Friar Timoteo, Friar Timothy. They go into the church where he is, and right then, he's with an older lady, and she says, "I don't really have time for a full confession today, although it always does my heart good. I just wanted to see how that grant I had given you to pray my husband out of purgatory is working."

"Oh, well, I think we are going to need a little bit more of a grant, but I mean, he's halfway out; his foot is on the step stone of Heaven."

"Here's some more money."

"Yes, thank you so much. Oh, these women are such silly creatures. The only things sillier are their husbands. Why, Messer Nicia, I have not seen you in many days in church. Your wife used to come day after day and pray; did anything ever come of it?"

"No, no, we still do not have the child. This is my friend I have brought with me; he's a famous doctor from France."

"Oh."

"Dr. Callimaco is my name."

"What can I do for you?"

"We've got a little bit of a situation here."

"Yes, yes, what is the situation?"

"One of my relatives is a very noble-born woman. She's not married, she's going to have a baby, and her family is distraught. Could we get a dispensation from you for her to have an abortion?"

"Oh, no, that takes a great deal of money."

"We're willing to pay a great deal of money."

"OK, I'll do it."

Then Ligurio runs off, comes back, and says to the priest, "Actually, we don't need that now. No, no, it has all been taken care of, but we have another question for you."

The friar says, "Aha, they just got me to go along with that one sin in order to come up with a bigger sin."

They lay out the whole plan. "The thing is," Messer Nicia says, "I would be so happy if this happened that I would be willing to make a huge donation to the church."

"How big?"

"Thousands of ducats."

"Thousands of ducats?"

"Yes, but I'd have to have a stipulation, Friar Timothy."

"What is that?"

"You alone, at your sole discretion, would expend it."

"Oh, yes, yes; well, I think we can perhaps look into this situation for you. Send Lucrezia to me."

Lucrezia comes; her mother-in-law is with her, and her mother is with her, her mother Sostrata. They come to the friar, and Lucrezia is saying, "I won't have anything to do with this."

The mother keeps saying, "We want a grandchild. If the friar tells you it's OK, will you do it?"

"Well, all right." So they do.

They get there and the friar explains, "Yes, this would be a little sin to sleep with another man. You'll get the potion, you'll sleep with this other man, he might die, but then, your husband will give you the baby."

She says, "I think this is a terrible sin."

"No, it's about the equivalent of eating meat on Friday; that's about it. We can wash it away."

"Really? Commit adultery and have somebody killed?"

"Yes, yes, I think so, for a thousand ducats—I mean, for the sake of God and having a new worshiper—yes, indeed."

All right, she's willing to do it, but now it's a little more complicated because Callimaco is the one who wants to sleep with Lucrezia—are you following all of this? Yet Messer Nicia has seen him, and he will think this is suspicious—that the doctor is willing to sleep with this lady and die—so there's something suspicious. They have to go through a huge ruse of getting Friar Timothy and themselves all in disguises to "capture" Callimaco in disguise so that Messer Nicia will not recognize him. There's Messer Nicia in a disguise, thinking he looks a little younger and slimmer these days than he used to, flattering himself. Then they go out in the dead of night, and there is this drunken student coming through the streets; that is, of course, Callimaco in disguise. Are you following this? Callimaco [is] in disguise, and they grab him, and snatch him, and carry him into the boudoir, and the task is done.

Messer Nicia, instead of being upset about this, makes sure it gets done right and makes sure it's done just the way it should [be], and then throws poor Callimaco out, and says, "All right, you drunken student, you got just what you deserved, hanging around the streets late at night. Now I hope you don't die, but you might."

He goes in to his wife, and she says, "Oh darling, at first I was very disturbed about this idea, but now I feel that it was just the right thing. Please tell me, how did you learn about this wonderful drug that you have given me that will give us so much choice?"

"Oh, well, the doctor."

"Callimaco?"

"Yes, the doctor, Callimaco."

"Oh, you know, I hope he will become a good friend of ours."

"Would you really like that?"

"Yes." This is because, of course, in the course of their night together, Callimaco has explained to Lady Lucrezia who he really is, and far from being upset, she has welcomed his embraces. But of course, the husband doesn't know that she knows who he is.

"I will have Messer Callimaco and his friend come by any time they want."

"Why darling, why don't you give Callimaco, the doctor, a key to our house? Because he's all alone and can come and have dinner whenever he wants."

"Oh, I like this idea wonderfully."

And so the little play comes to its end, a play of betrayal and adultery, but one that tickled the fancy of the age of the Renaissance and has continued to amuse audiences. Now my question always is, [first:] Is *The Mandragola*, or any play like this, a great book? How did we define a great book? It is a book that has a great theme, it is written in noble language, and it speaks across the ages. We also want it to speak to each of us individually. I don't think illicit love is a great theme. On the other hand, we had *Tristan and Isolde*, one of the most influential courtly love novels, and we saw how the whole ceremony of courtly love in the Middle Ages was built around illicit love. Novels like *Anna Karenina* may show the destructive quality of such illicit love, but many a person has been absolutely gripped by Tolstoy's tale of this lady so infatuated that she would throw away her life.

Is illicit love a great theme? The language of Machiavelli is certainly a good language, a noble language, very pure Italian. Does it speak across the ages? I do worry that many people who would be distressed at the frankness of Machiavelli watch very similar things on television and in movies today. That theme clearly speaks across the ages. But I also have another criterion I ponder for what makes a great book, and it is particularly relevant to Machiavelli's *The Prince*. Can a person with an evil mind write a truly great and noble book? We come back to *The Prince* (*Il Principe*) that Machiavelli wrote, that many see as the beginning of modern political thought. [It puts forth] this idea that there is no right and no wrong; that it is only what works that matters; that absolute expediency and success are the only criteria; and that honor, courage, justice—all that the Middle Ages viewed as the cardinal principles for a ruler—are pointless.

It's a book, of course, that Adolf Hitler owed the most to—he always had a copy on his nightstand—and that Joseph Stalin believed to be absolutely true. In *The Mandragola*, we see Machiavelli telling us again that fidelity in marriage means nothing, that trust between a husband and a wife means nothing, that everything is for sale, and that everybody has their price if they are going to get what they want. I think that it is a very evil message, [just] as *The Prince* may be an influential but a very evil book. But it bothers me that *The Prince* continues to speak across the ages, as do these situation comedies based on the same theme as *The Mandragola*. It is almost to say that one of life's lessons may unfortunately be that many people do always have their price; that evil seems to win out in the end; that even those that seem to be good, virtuous, and true do—if it is convenient and expedient for them—terrible, evil, destructive deeds. That is the lesson that Machiavelli offers us in his *Mandragola*, as he offered us in his *Prince*.

Lecture Twenty-Eight
Erasmus—*In Praise of Folly*

Scope:

"Vanity of vanities; all is vanity," said the author of Ecclesiastes. Absurdity is in the eye of the beholder. *In Praise of Folly* teaches us to step back and see ourselves as others see us. All that we take so seriously, our jobs, our professional reputations, even our fitness programs and diets, may one day be seen as nothing but vanity. We cannot live our lives as though nothing matters, but we should pause to laugh at ourselves and our follies.

Desiderius Erasmus was one of the greatest Humanists of Renaissance Europe. He devoted his life to study and writing. He explored the history and literature of Greece and Rome to free the minds of his contemporaries from what he regarded as the ignorance and superstition of the Middle Ages. Greece and Rome were, for him, the fountains of pure knowledge. He was also deeply religious and saw in the study of the Greeks the path to understanding the true meaning of Christianity. *In Praise of Folly* was written for his friend, and fellow Humanist, Thomas More in the form of classical orations. It appears to be a lighthearted satire on contemporary foibles, but it is, in reality, a sharp vehicle of irony to criticize social, moral, and cultural wrongs.

Outline

I.   We continue our exploration of the theme of irony, satire, and laughter with *In Praise of Folly* by Desiderius Erasmus (1469–1536). The work is a panegyric speech of praise in honor of this very theme.

II. Humanism was the essence of the Renaissance.

    A. The age of the Renaissance saw a rebirth in understanding of classical antiquity and a breaking away from the forms of the Middle Ages.

    B. Artists studied the use of perspective to gain an understanding of what Greek and Roman art had been able to achieve.

C. In the 14th century, with the demise of the Byzantine Empire, some Greek scholars made their way to Italy. This contact provided an opportunity for Humanists, such as Petrarch, to learn the Greek language.

III. Erasmus was one of the greatest Humanists.

    A. He was born in Rotterdam, probably the son of a priest who had an illicit relationship.

    B. When his parents died of the plague, Erasmus was sent to study at the school of the Brethren of the Common Life.

    C. Erasmus went on to study at some of the great universities of Europe.

    D. His book *Adages* was well received and earned a large sum of money.

    E. Erasmus had the idea to write a book on folly while traveling across the Alps. He spent some time with the English Humanist Thomas More, who was at the time considering putting aside scholarly matters to serve King Henry.

IV. At More's home in England, Erasmus tried to convince More to continue writing and stay out of politics. Erasmus began *In Praise of Folly* (the title in Greek is a play on More's name) while staying with More.

    A. The work begins with Folly, dressed as a clown, explaining her significance and power to a group of intellectuals, politicians, and literary figures.

    B. Part of Humanist learning was the ability to give a speech in honor of a public figure or at a funeral or christening. No one had yet given a speech in honor of Folly.

    C. Folly explains that she is responsible for the very existence of humanity.

    D. She describes her instrumental role in the creation of government and the organized exploitation of people.

    E. She tells us that she is responsible for the existence of lawyers, soldiers, professors, scientists, and theologians.

    F. Hobbies, as well, are the creations of Folly.

    G. Folly concludes by saying that she should be welcomed and even worshiped because she has made human life possible.

H. When the work was published, it outraged many in the professions mentioned, but none more so than theologians.

V. Erasmus's great contribution to the world of learning was his Greek New Testament.

> **A.** Erasmus was convinced that God had chosen him to learn Greek so that he could discover what the original versions of the New Testament actually said.

> **B.** In 1516, the Greek New Testament and its corresponding Latin translation were produced. Humanists hailed the work, especially those in northern Europe, where Humanism was deeply connected to the church and Christianity.

> **C.** One of the first readers of this New Testament in Greek was Martin Luther.

> **D.** Tasked with teaching a course on Paul's Letter to the Romans, Luther sat down with Erasmus's New Testament and began to puzzle over the question of grace versus works, faith versus deeds.

VI. The questions inspired by Erasmus's New Testament eventually led Martin Luther to tack his Ninety-five Theses to the door of a chapel in Wittenberg. When the Reformation began, Luther thought Erasmus would join him, but Erasmus refused in favor of maintaining order in society.

> **A.** Erasmus moved from town to town through the tumult of the Reformation, winning fans and friends.

> **B.** He died in the city of Basel, called the "fountainhead of the heresy" by many in the Catholic Church, and with many on the Protestant side claiming he was a coward and a turncoat.

VII. The life of Erasmus gives us one more good lesson: Tell the truth, and when the fanatics begin to fight, step back and be a force for moderation. Moderation may be the height of true wisdom.

Suggested Reading:

Erasmus, *In Praise of Folly*.

McConica, *Erasmus*.

Questions to Consider:

1. Can you write *In Praise of My Own Follies*?

2. Is the New Testament in Greek of Erasmus proof that scholarly ideas can change history?

Lecture Twenty-Eight—Transcript
Erasmus—*In Praise of Folly*

In this, our 28th lecture, we continue with our exploration of the life lessons that we learn from the great books and our theme of irony, satire, and laughter. We turn to a contemporary of Machiavelli, the prince of all Humanists, he was called—Erasmus of Rotterdam—and his work *In Praise of Folly*. Literally, [it's] a work giving a panegyric speech of praise in honor of our very topic of laughter, folly, and mirth.

Humanism was the very essence of the Renaissance. The Renaissance meant "rebirth," and it was the rebirth of an understanding of classical antiquity. It was a breaking with the forms of the Middle Ages. In architecture, the high Gothic ceilings, the pointed arches, and the stained glasses were replaced by the pure forms of Greek and Roman architecture. In art, there was an understanding of the use of perspective that carried the Italian artist back to an understanding of what Greek and Roman art had been able to achieve. Sculptors like Michelangelo sought to recapture the beauty of the human form that had been the essence of classical art.

It was the age in which the knowledge of Greek was reborn in Western Europe. With the collapse of the Roman Empire, Greek essentially was no longer studied or understood in most of Western Europe. There were a few people in Italy who knew it to correspond with the eastern Roman Empire, but on the whole, it just had died out, and that closed one whole gateway to the classical world. It also, interestingly enough, closed the understanding of the New Testament, and the whole of church doctrine in the Middle Ages rested upon the Latin translation—the Vulgate—which had come down from Saint Jerome.

But in the 14th century, due to contacts between Italy and the dying Byzantine Empire, some Greek scholars made their way to Italy. This was the opportunity these Humanists—like Petrarch, the poet—finally had to learn Greek. It became like a spiritual experience to learn this language that enabled you to commune directly with Aristotle, with Plato, the tragedies, to read the *Iliad* in the original. With the fall of Constantinople in 1453, there were a large number of Byzantine intellectuals who were completely out of jobs and fled, first to Italy and then up into Northern Europe, where they began to teach the language. By the end of the 15th century, it was taught at

Oxford and Paris and was even fundamentally reforming the curriculum at the universities in order to focus more directly on the lessons of classical antiquity and less on how the Middle Ages interpreted them.

Of these Humanists who took as their cue that man is the measure, none was greater than Erasmus. He was born maybe even in the same year as Machiavelli. Machiavelli is a Humanist, you understand; he studies the classics in order to illuminate the present. Erasmus was born in Rotterdam—what we would call Holland today—probably in 1469, just as Machiavelli had been born in Florence in that year. But Holland did not exist as a country; it was a province of the area called the Low Countries, which belonged to the house of Austria. That's really what kind of citizen Erasmus was.

He was not born wealthy and almost certainly was illegitimate. His father most likely was a priest who had an illicit relationship, and though Erasmus was always very shy about talking of these matters, probably Erasmus's original name was Gerrit Gerritzoon. But when his father and mother died of the plague—and they took care of him—a guardian stepped in, and he got a good education. He was sent to study at the school of the Brethren of the Common Life. This was a group of laymen in the Low Countries who had become so distressed at the corruption in the church and so critical of the church that they decided that a new generation had to be educated in one simple lesson: the simplicity of the life of Christ, that all of the elaborate dogma that had been built up, all the persecution of heretics, had nothing to do with the message of Jesus. In fact, they were skeptical that you really needed more of the Bible than just the Gospels: Live your life in imitation of Jesus; forgive everyone; do not make judgments on people; to the woman taken in adultery, say, "Go and sin no more"; and follow the pattern of the life of Christ. They were pacifists, always turning the other cheek, but they also understood that the new generation would have to be practical. The men who wanted their sons to be lawyers, medical doctors, [and] diplomats sent them to the schools of the Brethren of the Common Life, where they learned Latin—which was as important as knowing the computer today to getting ahead in the world—and where they got a good preparation for university. That is where Erasmus studied.

Like other great men we have learned about in this course, he did not like school either. He said one of his teachers was a driveling ram, and all they did was batter the information into your head and make you hate the great books you were supposed to love. But he made it through, and his knowledge of Latin was extremely good, and he decided to go into the church. He became the secretary to a bishop—he was valued for his knowledge—and the bishop agreed that he could be ordained but never have to preach and that he would go to university. He studied some in Paris, he studied some at the great university of Louvain in the Low Countries, and he would study at Oxford.

He was not a child prodigy; he was 30 before he began to publish his first books [and] 40 before he wrote anything of importance. He decided not to write until he had absolutely mastered Latin and [had] been able to spend as much time as he wanted to on Greek. But he needed money, and he first burst upon the scene of Europe in 1506 with a book entitled *Adages*, or *Quotations*. It was extremely well done and a very intelligent book to write, because that was a day where every speech to be taken seriously had to have some quotes in Greek and Latin; the trouble was, you didn't know Latin that well and almost no Greek. So this was a dictionary of quotations by headings, and you can go down and say, "What does Homer say about war? What does Demosthenes say about taxes?" There was the little quote you needed to work in. This was still important in the time of the Founders of our country, and many of the debates at the Constitutional Convention work in a little bit of Latin or a little bit of Greek. One of the Founders said he was not surprised that such liberties were being taken with the freedom of the American people when such liberties were taken with the language of a dead people like the Romans. Sometimes you got these mixed up, but nonetheless [the quotations were used quite often].

Erasmus made some real money from [the book] and was able, for the rest of his life—though offered many professorships, offered many positions of honor—just to live as an independent writer and make no commitments to any group, any prince. He did make good ties with various printing houses in Italy, who used him as an editor to work on the editions of the classics they wanted to bring out, particularly in Venice. But he had also traveled in England and made the acquaintance of the best of all the English Humanists, Thomas More.

In 1509, Erasmus was traveling back from Italy, crossing the Alps, when he had the idea of his next book. It was going to be a study of folly and [how] all the problems [of] the world had come about with folly. He was now a European figure; his name, Desiderius, means "the one who is beloved" and represents many of the Humanists who took Greek or Latin names. Erasmus also means "the beloved" in Greek—Desiderius being in Latin, Erasmus being in Greek. But it is also the name of a saint in the Catholic Church, and it may be that Erasmus was actually born on the feast day of Erasmus the saint. But that's his name now: Desiderius Erasmus from Rotterdam.

He gets this idea of writing a book on folly. He sails to England [and] spends some time with Thomas More, whom he admires enormously. It's at the very time—as we shall see in our next lecture—when Thomas More is seriously considering putting aside being a Humanist in order to serve King Henry. Erasmus had earlier met King Henry, who was quite a Greek and Latin scholar himself, and Erasmus tried to talk to his old friend, staying with him out in the country: "This is a very bad decision. I know you think you can change King Henry for the better; I know you think you can make a difference in politics, but just stay with your books. This is a critical moment in the very history of England. I believe we can also do something by curing the corruption of the church. You will master more by writing than you ever will by being in politics."

In the course of this, [Erasmus] began to write, resting there, having been a little bit ill with kidney stones, there at Thomas More's house in England. [He began to write] *Encomium Moriae*, which means *In Praise of Folly*, but it is also a play in Greek upon Thomas More's name. It means, "More, you are about to commit great folly." But everybody in history commits folly, and that is the theme of this work, written in magnificent Latin: *In Praise of Folly*.

It begins with Folly, the fool, dressed like a clown. She gets up in front of an audience—an audience of learned people, politicians, and literary figures—and immediately, they begin to chuckle because she has on this hat with bells on it, and big shoes, and she has a huge nose. Folly says: "You see how important I am? You are sitting their gravely, your arms all folded, and I step up here and you begin to relax just a little bit. That's how much joy I bring into the world. Do you know, despite all the good things I, Folly, have done for the human race, nobody has ever given a speech in my honor?" That was part of the Humanist learning: to be able to give a speech in honor of the prince, to be able to give a speech in honor of a churchman, be able to give a good speech at a funeral or at a christening. [Folly says:] "Nobody has ever given a speech about Folly, so I am going to tell you, if you'll just give me a few minutes, what I have done for mankind and why there ought to be a temple built to me, Folly. Step one: There would be no human race without me."

Now, you can't get mad at me; this is an important book. I just want to explain it to you. You cannot get mad at me for what Erasmus said; are you following me? [Folly continues:]

There would be no human race. Folly is the only thing that gets people to marry. Why in the world would you undergo all the harassment of being married, give up your freedom, enslave yourself? Then, having made that folly, nobody would have children except for me. I delude people into having children. Think about a child; think of a baby—what a demanding creature that is. Then, they get a little older, and they act very, very bad, and you put up with all of this because you say, "They'll take care of me in my old age." Well, they'll put you in an old folks' home; they'll never think about you; [and] they'll conspire against your estate. No, only folly could make babies come into this world, so the very human race is dependent upon me.

But secondly: Would we have any government without folly? Look at you sitting out there; some of you are kings. It is the greatest folly (1) to want to have a king and (2) to want to be a king. Folly. Why do we have kings? Because we say they are given by God: Henry, king by the grace of God, of England. Do you really think God in all his wisdom gives some paltry figure to be ruler over men? I'd like you to show me one king in history that was good enough to really say God gave him to us. They are the most avaricious group in the world. Very well do they take an eagle and put it on their scepter, because the eagle flies down and eats up everything; he's greedy and cannot be satiated.

And then who would want to be a king? All the worries, all the people who intrigue about you. So we could not start and even have government without the folly that grips the human mind. Would we have any lords and ladies like you? The only reason you are lords and ladies is that the mass of ordinary people somehow think it's a good idea to work and slave so you can be at leisure. Government is nothing more than an organized exploitation of plain people. They pay all these taxes so that you can ride around on fine horses, dress well, and claim you're taking care of the realm along with the king. All you are taking care of is fleecing these poor lambs, but their folly makes it possible, makes it possible for me to talk to you. So you'd have no government; you'd have no families; you'd have no human race; and you'd have no professions.

I've just got to tell you, and again, don't get mad at me: This is just Erasmus, although you might see why a lot of people got mad at him for writing this. [Here's Folly:]

You would have no professions; they all rest upon folly. [First,] doctors: They are probably the best paid people in our society, and it's all folly. People go to doctors again and again—they never get cured—or if they cure you, it is just chance. They say a lot of nonsense over you, [but] you get well on your own. But human folly really thinks it can live forever, and that if you keep going to the doctor, he'll find all the ways to cure you; you'll have preventive medicine and live forever, when it is just folly to be living anyway.

But the lawyers: I don't know how long lawyers have been a plague upon society [says Erasmus; I don't say this], but already, Cicero, Demosthenes, Aristophanes—they talk about the plague of lawyers. Aristophanes says that we Athenians are the most litigious people in the world. You get mad at your neighbor because he looked at you crosswise: "I want to sue him." You get mad at your company that has sold you some product because it wasn't what you expected: "I'm going to sue them." There were always lawyers—there were in Athens; there were in Rome—that would take your case.

Do you know one of the reasons I admire Thomas More [says Erasmus]? He is a lawyer—a very distinguished lawyer—and every time somebody comes in and says, "I want to sue that person," he says, "No, don't sue anybody. A lot of things can happen to you in court, and almost all of them are bad." And that is absolutely true. But generation after generation—well into the future—will pay huge fees to lawyers; they will undertake suits thinking that their honor has been outraged or thinking that they have been wronged financially. So the lawyers survive only because of the folly of people that (1) want to sue and (2) make all these laws that make it impossible not to live without breaking the law. You've got the government in cahoots with the lawyers; lawyers encourage the government to make all these laws so they can sue other people and make money.

Third—and I'm not going to leave them out—the soldiers: Every soldier owes his whole livelihood to me, Folly. Would there be wars without human folly? What is clear, going all the way back to Homer, is that no war ever solves anything, and every generation starts another war. Glory in war? That is the height of folly. How do you get glory by killing someone else? No, in a world [of] reason—which you claim really existed—people would simply sit down and say, "I don't care whether you possess that city or not; let's not go to war." But the soldier lives because of my influence: folly.

Oh, I'm not going to leave out the professors; don't you worry about that. They are the epitome of a wise man. I've got a question for you: Who ever wants a wise man at the party or a wise woman? They want me. Do you want somebody all sallow-faced, creaking and groaning, eaten up by books, or do you want me there? Have you ever had a drink with a wise man? They are the most boring people in the world. Why? Because they wasted their whole lives learning a lot of stuff that doesn't matter, and their whole self-identity [this is from the wise Humanist, Erasmus] is built into this knowledge of what is not important; he knows everything about what's not important. They will spend their nights poring over their books, and they are so delighted if they find one rare Greek form that nobody has ever discovered before. So they publish, because they've got to publish to show that they have real meaning to their lives, and they're so afraid that some other bone-dry scholar is going to publish this discovery before they do.

Oh, and the scientists: They are pure folly. Do they really think that they are going to understand the world or anybody is happier because they have understood the world?

Let's not leave out the theologians. They are the most pompous group in the world. There is nothing more simple than the life of Jesus: He came to Earth and he taught, "Do unto others as you would have them do unto you," that the only commandments are "Love your neighbor" and "Love God." They can't be content with that; they have to spin out an elaborate set of doctrines. They've got to worry about "How can Jesus be God the Father, God the Son, and the Holy Ghost?" Then, they've got to persecute people who don't follow them in these doctrines. Rather than turn the other cheek, you persecute and burn in the name of God. That's pure folly. Isn't that pure folly? Yes, to take a simple message like that and to transform it into an object that carries out hate.

I guess I've gone on enough about the professions. But even hobbies, [like] the hunter: What is more folly than getting all dressed up, arming yourself with a weapon, getting a bunch of hunting dogs, and running out and killing some poor bear? Chasing him through the forest, when you have plenty to eat yourself, and killing him, and you think that's a great deal. Or gamblers: [T]hat is pure folly to think that you're ever going to win, and yet they sit there, day after day, utterly addicted to gambling. All of the professions of life, government, even the hobbies—they are all a testimony to me, Folly. I conclude by saying, welcome me, build a temple to me, understand how I have made all of your lives possible, and please, don't ever go looking for true wisdom.

When [Erasmus] published this—the first edition finally came out in 1512—he made a lot of people mad at him and no more so than the theologians. They were the important figures of the day. The Humanist More chuckled at it a little bit, but he also warned Erasmus, "I know I encouraged you to bring this out, but you are going to make a lot of people slander your reputation." And so they did.

The Humanists said, "How can you betray this fount of knowledge? We spend our lives studying Greek and Latin so that we can educate young men and women to be better citizens and better individuals."

The theologians just said, "He's a heretic; that's all he is. We ought to catch him and burn him."

Fortunately, he traveled to Switzerland—which was a tolerant nation even in those days—and stayed largely in the city of Basel, and continued to work on what he viewed not as an incidental pleasure (*The Praise of Folly*) but his great contribution to the world of learning, and it was the Greek New Testament.

Erasmus was convinced that God had chosen him to learn Greek not as just a flower of knowledge, but so that he could go back and see what the original Gospels, letters of Paul, and the whole New Testament really said. For one thing, the manuscripts that had come down were quite corrupt, and immediately, as he began to read Greek manuscripts, [Erasmus] realized that the Vulgate—the work of

Saint Jerome that was the basis of all Catholic doctrine—was wrong in many places just based on faulty manuscript readings, scribes having copied down the wrong word. Then, there were some verses in the Vulgate, such as the story about the woman taken in adultery, which he could not find in the earliest Greek manuscripts. In 1516, he brought out his first edition of the Greek New Testament with a corresponding Latin translation. It was hailed by Humanists because while in Italy, Humanism tended to be a more secular undertaking, in Northern Europe, Humanism was deeply involved with the idea of the church and with the idea of Christianity. Humanism was Christian humanity, Christian Humanism.

One of the first readers of this New Testament in Greek was a professor and monk at the University of Wittenberg in Germany, Martin Luther. He had understood as a young man how important it was to learn Greek. He had studied with some of the best Greek scholars in Germany, and he was eager to get this New Greek Testament from Erasmus, whom he admired so very much, and learn what the New Testament really said. He had a special chance, because in the summer of 1517, only a few months after he had gotten the New Testament of Erasmus, Professor Luther was brought into the office of the dean of the university.

The dean of the university said, "Professor Luther, you're a very successful teacher; you're our most popular teacher; you're a very good administrator, and that is why I made you head of the department. You're a very good scholar, and I know you like to spend your time with teaching and scholarship, but I've got a task for you. You know Brother Paul is ill, and he will not be able to teach his course this semester. I want you to teach a course on Paul's Letter to the Romans."

"I would love to teach that, Dean, but I've not really studied that as much as I should."

"I know, and we're going to give you a summer grant to give you time to develop this new course."

Luther sat down with the New Testament that Erasmus had provided. As he began to read the letter of Paul to the Romans, he puzzled over and over again about the question of grace versus works, of faith versus deeds. He pulled off his shelves the books that had taught him theology, such as Thomas Aquinas, and there, it was quite clear that the doctrine of the church said that deeds are just as important as faith and grace. But that wasn't what Paul had actually written, and the Vulgate had not really rendered that clearly; in fact, it looked at though it had almost glided over that point, because Paul said, "By grace alone are ye saved, not by deeds, lest any man can boast." And yet the whole apparatus of the Catholic Church was based on this idea of deeds; in fact, the Catholic Church believed that morality was only possible because people believed they would be punished for evil deeds. Perhaps even worse for Luther, it was built into the financial structure of the universities and the Catholic Church, because a major means of raising funds was to sell indulgences. This meant you paid a certain amount of money, and the church could pray your ancestors out of hell, pray them into heaven, or they could pray [for] you.

At this point, the church was in a great deal of need because the pope wanted to build a new St. Peter's, a big building project; you've seen these on college campuses. There were these development officers—they were churchmen, but they were development officers—and they traveled all through Europe. One of them was coming down in October to Wittenberg to raise money. Luther said, "This is wrong." This professor—unknown outside of Wittenberg—on Halloween, the 31 of October 1517, armed by what he had learned from Erasmus, nailed to the door of the chapel a set of Ninety-five Theses that he wanted to debate with this professor and development officer. At the very heart was: Are you saved by works or only by grace?

It became a very celebrated case. Luther found himself, despite all his wishes, hauled before the imperial Parliament itself. Faced by the most learned doctors of the church, he was asked the question: "Do you hold to this heretical notion that you are saved by grace and faith alone?"

Holding his copy of Erasmus's New Testament, [Luther] said, "If you can show me in this, the real Greek, where I am wrong, then I will recant everything. Otherwise, *Hier stehe ich* ["here I stand"]. I can do nothing else. God save me, God help me." And the Reformation of the church began.

Immediately, Luther thought that Erasmus would join him; *Praise of Folly* had shown how critical Erasmus was of the failings of the church. But Erasmus said no: "We must have an order in society. I see nothing in the New Testament that says that the pope is not the successor of Peter. I think that you, Martin Luther, are unleashing all matter of social and political changes that will destroy the very fabric of lives. I will not join either side. I will try to mediate."

Of course, that's the best way to get into all sorts of trouble: to try to not take sides. But Erasmus was not only a learned man; he was a very shrewd man. All through the tumult of the Reformation, he managed to move from town to town, winning fans and friends, staying as long as he was welcomed. If the town became too fanatic for his choices, he would move on to another. [He] died at a ripe old age, living in the city of Basel, called the "fountainhead of the heresy" by many in the Catholic Church. Some of his books [were] on the forbidden list of index, and some [people]—like Luther—on the Protestant side, [were] angry at him and saying that he was a coward and a turncoat.

Maybe part of folly is really thinking you're going to make a true difference in a fight that vicious, where both sides have become so dogmatic. Erasmus himself gives us one more very good lesson: Tell the truth, and then when the fanatics begin their fight, step back and be a force for moderation. Moderation may be the height of true wisdom.

Lecture Twenty-Nine
Thomas More—*Utopia*

Scope:

Thomas More's *Utopia* teaches us again to step back and see ourselves as others see us. Erasmus conveyed this message on an individual level; More does it on a national and even transnational level. We are so proud of our culture and our values that we want to import them to other countries and impose them on other civilizations. But perhaps we should realize that true happiness and harmony can be found in ways that we have not even considered.

The life of Thomas More is itself a lesson. He was shaped by the great books we read. Like Plato, Seneca, and Boethius, he went into politics believing he could change things for the better. He ended up on the executioner's block, preferring death to the violation of his principles.

Utopia was written in happier days. Composed in Latin and published in 1516, *Utopia* describes a nation that has achieved harmony and good government essentially through communism. The title means "No Place," but More clearly intended his work as a serious criticism of the legal, political, and cultural institutions of his day, the very institutions in which he played such a leading part.

Outline

I. Continuing with our theme of laughter and irony, we look now at the second of two great Renaissance satires: *Utopia* of Thomas More (1478–1535).

   A. More was born in London. His father was a prominent and wealthy attorney who was determined that young Thomas would follow in his footsteps.

   B. More learned Latin at the age of six and was sent for a period to the court of the archbishop of Canterbury, John Morton. Morton was also lord high chancellor of England under Henry VII.

   C. In addition to advanced Latin and Greek, More learned how to handle administrative duties during his tenure at Morton's court.

D. He was then sent to Oxford, where he studied the classics and the history of Greece and Rome.

E. More believed that the study of Greek and Latin could open new worlds for humanity. His father, however, was determined that More would not be a professor and sent him to law school in London.

F. More met Erasmus at the lord mayor of London's residence, and the two formed a fast friendship.

G. More loved learning but was also attracted to politics and power. He came to the attention of King Henry VIII, who surrounded himself with men who knew Greek and Latin because he believed they understood the practical applications of lessons from the classical past.

H. More rose rapidly in King Henry's court and was sent on numerous sensitive diplomatic missions.

II. More began to write *Utopia* while staying in the Low Countries after concluding negotiations with the Holy Roman Emperor.

    A. The work begins with a factual statement: While staying with Peter Giles, a friend in Antwerp, More meets a man named Raphael Hythloday.

    B. Giles introduces Hythloday as the most interesting man he knows and asks him to spend the morning speaking about the things he has seen.

    C. Hythloday describes a voyage with Amerigo Vespucci and his encounter with a land called Utopia.

    D. More asks Hythloday if he has considered becoming an adviser to the king, and Hythloday explains how foolish it would be to do so. He claims that he would advise the king to get rid of all private property because greed and money are the roots of all evil.

    E. Hythloday says that he once tried to persuade Lord Morton to accept his views regarding property and social justice. He tells More that he got his ideas from living among the Utopians.

III. Hythloday (whose name means "purveyor of nonsense") claims that Utopia is a real place. It is a large island that was settled almost 2,000 years ago by King Utopos.

- **A.** Utopos understood that monarchy was not a good form of government; thus, almost from the outset, Utopia is organized into 54 democratically governed cities.

- **B.** All political meetings in Utopia are held publicly, and every citizen has a voice in discussing issues.

- **C.** Each city is divided into two major parts; one part is farmland and the other is the land within the city.

- **D.** Farming is done voluntarily, and so much food is produced that no one has to pay for it.

- **E.** Households move every 10 years, and all goods are provided free of charge.

- **F.** Daily schedules are loose; citizens work six hours a day.

- **G.** Every citizen learns a trade that produces some type of item, and citizens have the freedom to learn new trades at will.

- **H.** The citizens of Utopia believe in one God and the immortality of the soul. They also believe in an afterlife that rewards good deeds and punishes evil deeds. No one, however, is forced to believe anything.

- **I.** Utopia has very little crime, and punishment is gentle and geared toward learning and rehabilitation.

- **J.** Having listened to Hythloday, More claims that he would love to see such things in his own land but does not believe it is possible.

IV. More sent *Utopia* to Erasmus, who saw to its publication in 1516. King Henry was so delighted with the work that he offered More the position of speaker of Parliament, which he accepted despite the warnings of Erasmus.

- **A.** More helped King Henry gain power in Europe, win recognition from the pope, and persecute heretics.

- **B.** On the condition that he help King Henry win an annulment of his marriage, More assumed the title of lord high chancellor of the king of England.

- **C.** By 1532, it was clear that More could not achieve Henry's annulment on the terms he wanted.

D. After continually refusing to swear an oath of allegiance acknowledging the king as head of the church, More was imprisoned and executed.

Suggested Reading:

Ackroyd, *The Life of Thomas More*.

More, *Utopia*.

Questions to Consider:

1. More argues that criminality is the fault of society, not the individual criminal. Do you agree?

2. The true objection to communism is that it is the violation of the right of property, which is as much an absolute right as life, liberty, and the pursuit of happiness. Do you agree?

Lecture Twenty-Nine—Transcript
Thomas More—*Utopia*

We come to the 29th of our lectures exploring the life lessons that we learn from the great books, and we continue with our theme in this section of laughter and irony. "To play seriously"; that is what the Humanists like Erasmus called the use of irony and satire to make important political, social, and intellectual points. *Encomium Moriae* (*In Praise of Folly*)—we examined it in our last lecture, but it also means "in praise of More" (*Moriae encomium*): Thomas More, the great friend of Erasmus. The *Praise of Folly* was actually written in Thomas More's house during one of the many visits between these two great Humanists.

We look now at the second of these great Renaissance satires, the *Utopia* of Thomas More. More was born in London in 1478, in the very center of London, in Milk Street. His father did not come from an aristocratic background, but he had made a great deal of himself and had become an extremely prominent and wealthy attorney, and he was determined that young Thomas would follow in his footsteps as an attorney. Thomas went to grammar school, where he learned Latin at the age of six; he would become one of the finest Latin stylists of his day. His father then sent him for a period to the court of the archbishop of Canterbury, John Morton. Morton was also lord high chancellor of England under Henry VII; this was the second most important position in the entire realm of England, the chief administrator of the king himself.

Henry VII had come to the kingship through civil war. In 1485, Henry had triumphed at the Battle of Bosworth Field, and he was absolutely determined that England would not have another civil war and that there would be an heir to the throne. He had produced his son, Henry VIII, and Henry VIII, in fact, received a very good classical background, learning Greek and Latin very well. There at the court of the archbishop of Canterbury and the lord high chancellor of England, Cardinal Morton, Thomas More learned not only more Greek and Latin, but he also learned how you handle yourself in administrative posts.

He was then sent on to Oxford, where he became absolutely enamored of the study of Greek and Latin, and this study of Greek and Latin opened up whole new worlds for that generation. It became the validation of an entire approach to politics, art, and literature. The classics of Greece and Rome, the history of Greece and Rome, the manner of approaching the texts of Latin and Greek authors—all of this transformed learning, and politics [was] seen as the mechanism by which you apply the lessons of the classical past to the present. You went back and actually examined the manuscripts and learned wherein important classical texts had been altered. This was then applied to religion itself, and the New Testament came under close scrutiny—and the manuscripts of the New Testament—as more and more scholars at more and more universities learned Greek.

More believed that in the study of Greek conveyed by the Latin language, a whole new world could be gained. But his father was determined he was not going to be a professor, and he sent him to law school, studying in London, and he became a very good attorney. It was during this period, when he was beginning his legal career, that he first met Erasmus. Erasmus was already a prominent Humanist, and the Humanists of those days—these scholars—had a fame that we can barely imagine today for someone who knows Greek or Latin. There are other academics in fields like economics that matter to us the way Greek and Latin mattered to the age of the Renaissance [and] gained such great fame. Erasmus was a European figure, and he was dining at a table at the lord mayor of London's residence. He was seated next to this young man—handsome young man, he described him—blond haired, blue eyed, fair complexion, and they began to speak in Latin. After a moment or so, Erasmus said, "*Aut tu Morus es aut nullus*." ("You are either More or nobody at all"), and More answered and said, "*Aut tu Erasmus es aut Diabolus*." ("You are either Erasmus or the devil himself"). And so they formed their fast friendship.

But in writing *The Praise of Folly* and dedicating it to Thomas More, Erasmus was already pointing out to his friend the possibly perilous path that More was trying to follow: to be both a scholar and a man of practical affairs and to enter into politics. But politics, the world of power—it just drew Thomas More. He had thought for a while of actually becoming a monk; he had lived for four years in a monastery and he regularly wore, even when he was lord high chancellor of England, a hair shirt. On Fridays, he would scourge himself. But he decided that the path of a monk was not for him. He had married, he had four daughters, and then he married again after his first wife died and had a stepchild by her, as well as they adopted a young girl, so he had six children in his household. He was a very devoted family man. In fact, he would never get angry with his children, and if they finally exasperated him, he would spank them by whipping them with a peacock feather; that's as strong as he would get. He loved his family, he loved his learning, but he also loved power. He was most attractive to King Henry VIII, who had come to the throne in 1509.

Henry liked to surround himself with men who knew Greek and Latin, not for their ornaments of learning, but because they practically understood the use of the classical past. They had ideas about power gleaned from not only Cicero but from Thucydides that could be applied to the realpolitik of the day. Thomas rose very rapidly in the appreciation of Henry. He had become a very wealthy lawyer, but he was also elected undersheriff of London [and] entered Parliament. By 1515, King Henry was sending Thomas More on numerous very delicate negotiating missions, particularly to the Low Countries—to Holland and to Belgium—to negotiate not only matters of trade but also matters of high politics with the emperor of the Holy Roman Empire, Charles V.

It was there that More found himself in 1515 with a few months on his hands. The negotiations had been concluded over a trade agreement with the Low Countries to receive the wool of England. They had been concluded very satisfactorily and very rapidly, and he had about three or four months to spend some time in the Low Countries. He was staying with a very erudite young scholar named Peter Giles, who like More, was also involved in politics. There, they began to talk about what the ideal commonwealth would be, and it was there that More came upon his idea to write *Utopia*. He began it there in the house of Peter Giles in Antwerp and described this place, which from its Greek title means "nowhere," *ou* ("no") *topia*—nowhere.

The work begins as a factual statement. It says that "I, Thomas More, was there in Antwerp, staying with my good friend Peter Giles, and one day we had gone to mass, we were coming home, and he ran into an old acquaintance, Raphael Hythloday—Raphael, like the messenger from the Old Testament, and Hythloday, a Greek coinage that means "purveyor of nonsense."

Giles says, "More, I want you to meet Hythloday; he is the most interesting man you can talk to today. He has traveled to places not only that are far away, but no one but Hythloday himself has ever seen."

"I would enjoy that enormously."

Giles said, "Come to us and spend the late morning with us, Hythloday, and explain to More all the things that you have seen." They settle in for a long discussion there in the home of Peter Giles.

Hythloday says, "Yes, I was very fortunate. I traveled with the great Amerigo Vespucci. I went on his third and fourth voyages to the New World. But he went on even beyond the New World, and at his farthest points he put 24 of us, and we then got permission to go on even further, and so on and on we sailed. At first, the climate was desert-like, and then it was very hot, but then we reached an extremely temperate climate and a land filled with beautiful cities, and we were there in this land called Utopia."

More now interrupts and says, "Now what, do tell me, [do] you do?"

Hythloday says, "I do very little; I simply ponder the learning I have."

More says, "Why, you should become an adviser to the king. You are a man of enormous learning and all this experience, these places you have been."

Hythloday says, "That is the most foolish idea—if you will excuse me—I have ever heard. Why would anyone of learning, intelligence, and insight become the adviser to a king and get involved in politics? Surely you're not going to do that, Thomas More."

"I was going to give it some thought."

"It is a very bad idea. First of all, kings do not want any advice." (You might think of becoming a staff member to a politician today.) "They don't really want advice; they want yes-men" ([and] yes-women, we would say today) "who will tell them what they want to hear and then find a way to do it no matter how disreputable the idea of the king is. Of course, More, why would I—Hythloday—be able to give any advice to a king, since most of them want to make wars? That is what they are really interested in, whether it is the king of France, the king of England, [or] the Holy Roman Emperor. They can't rule the country they already have, but they want to take over somebody else's country and ruin it just as well. I know nothing about war, and besides, no honest man—you've read your Plato, haven't you, More?—Socrates says, can survive in politics; it is too corrupt. [Imagine] you were on a council, and the king actually listened to you, and you gave him sound advice, such as, 'What does it matter whether or not you rule France? You are king of England; take care of England.' Even if he listened to that, the other mediocrities around the table would destroy you, because mediocrity cannot stand excellence. They would find a way, first, to undermine you and, then, to have you killed. So no, I would not want to be a king, but if I were an adviser to a king, or if I were even a king, I would say the following: that most of the world's problems come from private property. Greed and money are the root of almost all evil, and I would advise the king to get rid of all private property."

"Have you ever advised the king to do that?"

"No, no, no, but I did once, since you asked me this, More. I did once advise the lord high chancellor of England to do that."

"Who was it?"

"John Morton."

"Why, he was the hero of my youth; he's the wisest man I ever knew."

"One day, I was dining with him, and one of his bishops came in and said he felt so good coming to dinner that evening because he had passed 20 thieves hanging on the gallows. We were really enforcing law and order in England. I said, 'How many did you see last week?'

"'Oh, I think I saw only 14 last week hanging from the gallows.'

"'Ah, you see, so you hang 14 last week, and there were 20 to hang this week; don't you think it's curious that you are enforcing law and order, but you have to keep hanging people and more and more people?'

"'That's the only way people learn, by hanging them.'

"'What if instead of hanging men for stealing, you stop the reasons for stealing?' All the advisers to the archbishop began to pipe up and say what a dumb idea this was, but the archbishop was a man who liked learning and liked wisdom, and he told them, 'You shut up; *docuday*; be silent. Let Hythloday speak.'

"I said, 'Don't you understand that all government everywhere is nothing but a conspiracy between the wealthy to rob the poor? Poor people in this country have to steal to feed their families. They're not poor; they don't want to be poor in the sense of beggars; they want to be productive: They want to be productive carpenters, masons, weavers, farmers. But you tax them so heavily, just to support your luxurious wealthy class, that they are destroyed. Or talk about the economic transformation that has swept England. Sheep are the most passive of all animals, and yet they are destroying thousands of human beings. Your wealthy decided they can make more money by enclosing their lands and raising sheep, and so they turned out of their homes—[let's say "downsized" today]—they downsized thousands of individuals, hundreds on each large farm that had worked there for generations. They just fired them to cut their expenses and to increase profits. Now sheep roam the lands where ordinary farmers used to live, and these farmers are turned out onto the roads. Yes, to feed their families they steal, and you then hang them. That is what you call social justice?' So you see, More, that's the kind of advice I give, and it makes me not very popular."

"Where did you get this idea," Thomas More asked, "that private property is the root of all evil?"

"I got it from living among the Utopians."

"Really?"

"That is the best-ordered society I have ever seen."

"Tell us more about it."

"I will go on for a long time and I'm hungry, I have to tell you."

"Let's have lunch," interjects Peter Giles. "We'll have lunch, and after luncheon, we'll continue our talk out here in the garden." They eat and then they continue their talk.

Hythloday says (now remember, he's a purveyor of nonsense): "Utopia is a real place. It's a large island; very well defended by nature; a good harbor, but one that is easily defended; and it was originally settled almost 2,000 years ago by King Utopos. But he understood that monarchy was not a good form of government, that it should be a free government. And almost from the outset, like the classical Greeks, the people of Utopia have been free citizens, governing themselves democratically in their own individual cities.

"There are 54 of these cities on the island of Utopia, each independent in its own way but following voluntarily the same way of life, the same structures of government. Those structures of government rest upon the fact that there is no property held in common whatsoever. Their governments are democratically elected: Each household contributes one vote; each household votes together, and they elect a certain number of philarchs, they are called—supervisors—who serve a one-year term. Then, all of the supervisors elect a governor, and then, all the governors elect the general governor of all of Utopia. They come together on a regular basis in a senate and discuss all matters that come before them. The super-governor can rule as long as he lives, as long as he does not conspire to take over power. They govern themselves under laws that they give themselves. They have very good regulations for the operation of their senate. Any item that is introduced on one day, they must wait at least until the next day to vote it so that nothing is pushed through. All of their meetings are in public—not like the Star Chamber of your king—but all the meetings are in public, and everyone has a say and can discuss and supervise any issue that comes about. So they govern themselves under their own laws.

"Each city is divided into two major parts—one of them is the farmland, and one is the land within the city—and the cities are very well fortified. They believe in protecting themselves. They cannot be free unless they can protect themselves, so they have strong walls. But outside are the farmlands, and the farms are run by large households, and every two years, large numbers of people voluntarily go out to these farms, and there, they labor for two years. At the end of the first year, those who have already been out there two years come back into town, and that way, there is always a number of people there who know how to farm. You farm on that next year; then you go back to town. Unless, however, you find farming to be good for you; then you can stay on as long as you want to. They produce freely, by this system of amateur farmers, so much food that food is free in Utopia. No one pays for it.

"Inside the town, there are wonderful houses with large gardens, and every 10 years, each household changes its own house, so you don't become attached to your house. All the houses are built exactly the same—they are very well built—and each 10 years, you move to another house; somebody moves into your house. When you want food or any item, [such as] clothing, you simply go down to the local market, pick whatever you want, and bring it home. Nobody ever takes more than they need; why should they? Everything is freely provided. Their meals are taken in large public dining halls; the food is superbly cooked. No one is forced to come and eat in the communal dining halls, but why wouldn't you? The food is free; very, very well prepared; and there's wonderful companionship. They begin always with a reading of some moral tract, but they don't read too much lest it get boring; there's good conversation. The children are all lined up around the walls watching their elders eat so that they will learn good manners and how to be respectful. Then in the evening, you retire to your home.

"You don't need to get up too early the next morning [unlike people today, who are up at 5:00 a.m., exercising]. No, in Utopia, you woke up about 9:00. If you wanted to get up earlier, you could. There were a lot of interesting lectures, and a scholar might be giving a lecture early in the morning and you would go to it. Then, you went to work at 9:00, and you worked from 9:00–12:00, then you had a two-hour luncheon, and then 2:00–5:00, and then you came home. Yes, they work only six hours a day, but because everything is so well provided and everybody works with such a good heart, it all turns out well.

"Everyone has a trade. Even those who are in the political life still have a trade, and it's a real trade. It's not like a stockbroker; it is a trade such as a carpenter, a mason. You could be a clothier, you can weave, [be] an ironsmith—all of these are good, solid trades that produce actual items. Because they have everything in common—don't you see, More?—everyone is happy, and there is no greed. Everyone gets to do just what they like. Your father was an ironsmith, and he wants you to be an ironsmith; you try it for a while and you say, 'Dad, I'd like to be a scholar. I'd like to be one of those Utopians who spend their whole life just studying.' You go and talk it over with the governors, and they say, 'We believe the boy has what it takes, or the girl.' You can study to be a scholar, and then you spend your whole life studying these marvelous books."

"What kind of books do they read?"

"Without any help from us, they had already developed all the philosophical concepts we have, but we brought them Greek books, and they fell in love with Plato. They saw in his *Republic* the statement of their own ideal commonwealth."

"Do they have a religion?"

"Yes, they believe in one God; they believe that the soul is immortal; they believe that after life, you will be rewarded for good deeds and punished for evil deeds. But they do not force anyone to believe anything. 'There are many ways to God,' the Utopians say. 'Let each person follow his own way.'"

"Did you talk to them about Christianity?"

"We did, and many of them admired Jesus. They wondered, however, about our elaborate church ceremonies and all the squabbles that occur over doctrine here in Europe, people putting each other to death over what they believe. They thought Jesus' life was just perfect and was like theirs: 'Do unto others as you would have them do unto you.' They read with particular interest the book of Acts and how the early Christian community held all their goods in common. Yes, many of them converted to Christianity, and no one had an objection to it."

"Do they have crime?"

"Very, very little crime, and those who do commit crime—unless it's terribly heinous—are punished in a very gentle way that allows them to learn and reform themselves. Holding everything, however, in common, there is very little reason for anyone to steal, to be jealous, or to murder anyone."

"Well," More said, "having listened to this wonderful description of Utopia from you, Raphael, like a messenger from God himself, I can only say that I would wish to see these things in place. However, I never expect that they will be in place."

More wrote his *Utopia* and sent it off to Erasmus. So confident was More in the opinion of Erasmus that he wasn't going to publish it unless Erasmus thought it was worthwhile, and Erasmus was delighted with this wonderful satire and saw to its publication in the year 1516. King Henry read it and thought it was marvelous, laughed all the way through, and said, "Very profound in all of your thoughts, Master More. Now, how would you like to be speaker of Parliament?"

In 1523, under the leadership of King Henry and aided by Cardinal Wolsey, the lord high chancellor of the king of England, Thomas More became the speaker of Parliament. Once again, there was this tug in his heart between just spending his life in learning or power. The more power he got, the more he deluded himself to believe [the opposite of what] Erasmus kept writing him: "It is a deadly road that you are on." But there was something about the beautiful robes that he wore; the elaborate gold medals around his neck, given to him as a sign of the king's favor; sitting at the highest table in the great banquets, even though there was a hair shirt under him, that made More feel he could really change the world.

He had already helped King Henry in 1519. In 1517, as we saw in our last lecture, Luther had published his Ninety-five Theses. Immediately, Henry entered the fray and, aided by More, wrote an attack upon Luther and won from the pope the title "Defender of the Faith." More helped King Henry gain power in Europe, gain recognition from the pope, and persecute these heretics. They were attempting to overthrow millennia of tradition and the sacraments of the holy church.

[In] 1523, [More was] speaker of Parliament. Then, in 1529, the king came to Thomas and said, "More, I have another suggestion for you. Would you like to be lord high chancellor of England?"

"Oh, your majesty has already loaded me down with so many honors."

"Yes, I know, but it has turned out most unfortunately. Wolsey could not handle the great matter I put before him."

"Your majesty, I don't know if any man could successfully have handled that."

"Yes, but you know I must divorce the queen, Catherine. She cannot give me a son, and without a son—an heir—England will be plunged into civil war. I cannot allow that. That alone determines my actions. All these scurrilous rumors that I am in love with Anne Boleyn, that amounts to nothing. But I must have a wife who can give me a son, and I must have a lord high chancellor who can gain the pope's assent to annul the marriage that I have made with Catherine. You agree that marriage was incestuous, don't you, More?"

"I think it could be read that way, your majesty."

"She was the wife of my own brother; they were wedded and bedded, More, I tell you. I never should have married her in the first place. The pope was wrong to give me an annulment to marry her."

"Yes, your majesty, but …"

"Handle the great matter for me, More; you will never be sorry."

So More accepted the lord high chancellorship, and for three years, he did his best to keep his faith with the king and, at the same time, to keep his faith with the church. For this man who loved power so much nonetheless deeply believed that the pope was the vicar of Christ on Earth, that Jesus had established, through Peter, the bishop of Rome as the source of authority. He could not believe that an earthly king could hold that position. By 1532, it was clear he could not achieve the annulment on the terms that he—More—wanted.

He went to see the king, and the king smiled and said, "I know you've done your best, More. You have been a true servant to me, and if I can ever help you do anything for your honor or profit, just let me know."

Have you ever failed your boss in anything, and he smiled as he took back the job, and you knew you were finished? More knew he was finished. He was too powerful, too well known, and his support too important. The king's men kept hounding him, even after he had laid down his office and retired to private life. "You must swear this oath of allegiance that every clergyman in England is swearing, that every citizen is swearing: that the king is the head of the church."

More would not do so. "I blame no man," he said, "who does swear it, but I cannot."

After interrogation after interrogation, he was put into the Tower of London. The king himself implored More, "Just sign this piece of paper saying that I am king as well as head of the church."

More's wife found her husband's position utterly foolish. "Sign a piece of paper for the good of your children, for my good." He would not.

On July 7, having spent months in the Tower of London, haggard but unbroken, he marched to the scaffold. He gave a gold sovereign to the executioner and said, "When you strike, my neck is short; please make a good job of it and try not to cut the beard I have grown. I like it so much." Then he looked out to the crowd as he knelt down, the king's good servant but God's first.

The executioner struck the blow and the head fell into the basket, was raised up with a shout—"Behold the head of a traitor"—placed upon a pike, and set upon London Bridge.

Lecture Thirty
George Orwell—*Animal Farm*

Scope:

Animal Farm teaches us about the potential of reform to deteriorate into totalitarianism—and not necessarily national reform but the reform of any human institution: a volunteer organization, a single church, a corporation, or a university. All institutions are flawed because humans are flawed. Plato, Seneca, Boethius, and Thomas More knew that, but they still became involved in politics and government. Others of us will do the same, but Orwell warns us with the allegory of Manor Farm.

George Orwell was the pen name of Eric Blair. In his own words, his writings were directed against every form of totalitarianism. *Animal Farm* is a biting satire of why the Russian Revolution went so catastrophically wrong. The animals, motivated by the highest principles of communism and equality, seize control of Manor Farm. They set up an animal paradise. But one by one, each of the seven commandments of the animal revolution is diminished. History is rewritten. Lies become the truth. Driven by the lust for power, greed, and self-aggrandizement, a small clique of thuggish pigs imposes a reign of brutality, terror, and starvation. The old regime of humans was haphazard in its cruelty and exploitation. It took animals to create a state of systematic totalitarian exploitation and cruelty for their fellows.

Outline

I.   We come to the last of our lectures on the theme of laughter and irony. Our last novel in this section is George Orwell's *Animal Farm*, which addresses questions regarding injustice in general and the role of private property in the existence of injustice.

   A.   Plato believed that private property is the cause of much of the absence of morality in the world. He constructed his ideal commonwealth on the absence of private property.

   B.   According to Plato, the key to ridding the world of private property was to educate young people so that they would enjoy all things in common.

C. The greatest single experiment in holding private property in common was the Soviet Union, and Orwell explores this system in his book *Animal Farm*.

II. Orwell (1903–1950) was born Eric Arthur Blair into what he described as a "lower upper-middle class" family.

    A. Orwell's father was a civil servant in India, and the family was determined that he would have a good education.

    B. Orwell was educated at Eton but failed to get a scholarship to Oxford, and his family could not afford to send him.

    C. Orwell joined the Indian police force but found it miserable and resigned after a few years. He had a deep suspicion of bureaucracy and wanted to become a novelist. He had difficulty publishing his material and endured financial hardship while living in London and Paris.

    D. Orwell was in his mid-30s when the Spanish Civil War broke out. He considered the war to be an embodiment of the struggle between the forces of good and the forces of totalitarian government.

III. Like many intellectuals of the time, Orwell was blind to the true nature of the Soviet government. Throughout the 19th century, socialist thinkers had debated the question of how to get rid of private property; thus, the Soviet government began in a great burst of hope.

    A. The works of Karl Marx and his communist view took on the force of a religion.

    B. In 1917, the dream of a communist government became a reality when the Bolsheviks seized power in Russia.

    C. By the time the Soviet government began to coalesce and emerge as a power in 1922, liberal intellectuals around the world looked on the establishment of communism as the dawning of a new age.

    D. The revolutionary leader Lenin died in 1924; a struggle for his legacy began between Joseph Stalin and Leon Trotsky.

    E. By 1927, Stalin had carefully consolidated power, and Trotsky was exiled, first to Siberia, then to Mexico.

F. Stalin became absolute master of the Soviet Empire, and a new generation was educated in the principles and practices of communism.

G. In 1941, invaded by Hitler, Stalin proved strong enough to win the Great Patriotic War.

IV. Orwell published *Animal Farm* in 1945, while Stalin stood at the absolute peak of his power. Orwell dedicated his writing to exposing the evils of totalitarianism.

A. Orwell had joined the republican forces during the Spanish Civil War, thinking that he was fighting against fascism. There, he learned from communist troops that Stalin and Hitler were simply two sides of the same coin, both devoted only to power.

B. *Animal Farm* is about the brave hopes that had been raised with the abolition of private property or, in this case, the tyranny of man.

C. The story begins at Manor Farm in England. The animals have gathered to listen to old Major, a pig, describe a vision he has had in which the farm is taken over by the animals.

D. Major describes the exploitation the animals regularly experience at the hands of Mr. Jones, the farmer. Though Major knows he is close to death, he entreats the other animals to pursue his dream.

E. The dream is kept alive after Major's death, and the animals work to realize it. The pigs begin to develop a doctrine called Animalism, which scientifically proves that animals are smarter than humans. They assert that when human order collapses, the animals will establish a great cooperative state.

F. The animals develop a series of commandments based ultimately on the idea that all animals are equal and are superior to humans.

G. Eventually, the animals riot and the humans are driven from the farm. The farm is renamed "Animal Farm," and a provisional government is established under the leadership of the pigs Snowball and Napoleon.

H. The animals learn to read and write and form committees to solve the farm's problems.

I. When it becomes clear the Animal Farm is not on the verge of collapse, the local farmers attack. The animals win the battle, and the farm is left alone.

V. The animals continue to live in relative harmony, until the pig Napoleon suddenly seizes power from Snowball with a pack of dogs he has raised. Napoleon assumes complete control.

    A. Napoleon begins to rewrite history (as was done in the old Soviet Union) when he insists on the construction of a windmill that had been proposed by Snowball. Napoleon now claims that Snowball had been opposed to the idea but that he is in favor of it.

    B. When the windmill collapses, Napoleon blames Snowball and his collaborationists. The collaborationists are killed, as is an animal who calls attention to the fact that Napoleon has now violated one of the most important commandments established by the animals.

    C. Napoleon continues to revise the commandments in favor of the pigs. Ultimately, he plans to turn the farm into a capitalist venture, and the other animals suffer as a result.

    D. The animals eventually witness the pigs and humans consorting around a table, drinking and playing cards. They can no longer distinguish between the two species.

    E. Napoleon proclaims that "Animal Farm" has been and always will be "Manor Farm." The animals return to the barn to find all of their commandments altered, most significantly the last one. What had once read, "All animals are equal," now includes the addendum "but some animals are more equal than others."

Suggested Reading:

Bloom, *George Orwell*.

Hammond, *An Orwell Companion*.

Orwell, *Animal Farm*.

Questions to Consider:

1. The chief pig is named Napoleon. Does this suggest that the Russian Revolution is not the only revolution to end badly?

2. Does *Animal Farm* reflect any of your personal experience in reform movements?

Lecture Thirty—Transcript
George Orwell—*Animal Farm*

In this, our 30th lecture, we continue our exploration of the life lessons that we learn from the great books, and we come to the last of our lectures on our theme of laughter and irony. We saw in our last lecture how Thomas More used laughter, irony, and satire to explore the question: Why does injustice exist? The lesson for life is most certainly that injustice exists. Good people have bad things happen to them; wealthy, powerful people seem to commit wrong after wrong with no punishment being given to them. A cynic might still ask, with More or his friend Hythloday, whether government is indeed just a giant conspiracy to plunder the productive people. Our last novel is George Orwell's *Animal Farm,* which also asks the questions: Why does injustice exist; what can be done about it; and is private property the reason for all this injustice?

It is a question that goes back to the very essence of the classical tradition of the great books. Cicero, in his *De officiis*—his book *On Moral Duties*—believed that private property and respect for private property [were] the very foundations of justice and that no morality could exist without private property. On the other hand, Plato said, no, private property is indeed the cause for much of the absence of morality, the injustice in the world. Plato constructed his ideal commonwealth on the absence of private property. He believed in it so deeply that at one point in his life, he was offered a very large consulting fee to give laws to a new city that was being founded, Megalopolis. His first question to the committee who came to ask him to give them their laws was: "Are you going to have private property?"

The committee said, "Of course, we are."

"Then," Plato said, "I will have nothing to do with it because no laws will work and give justice if you have private property."

That is how deeply Plato believed that private property was evil. The question, though, is—and was asked to Plato—how can you get rid of private property? Plato's view was that you can educate; with the new generation, you start with the young and you educate them not to have private property but to enjoy all things in common. This, of course, was also what the early church tried to do, to hold all things in common, but they found it failed. Thomas More, too, believed that all things could be held in common if citizens were educated the way the citizens of Utopia were: to work together from the very beginning, to dine together, to raise their children together.

But the greatest single experiment in holding property in common was the Soviet Union. [For] an exploration of whether the Soviet Union demonstrated that all good things will flow from an absence of private property, George Orwell wrote his brilliant book, *Animal Farm*. It continues in the path of Aristophanes in its biting social satire. Like [the work of] Aristophanes, *Animal Farm* is funny, but there is a bitter, bitter tinge to the funny happenings in the story.

Orwell was born Eric Arthur Blair, and that is, in fact, the name he wanted to be buried under, as well. He was born in 1903. He described his family as "lower upper-middle class." His father was a civil servant in India in those days when India was the jewel in the crown of the British Empire. The family was determined that young Eric would have a good education. He finally ended up at school in Eton, where one of his tutors in French was Aldous Huxley, whose *Brave New World* we studied. But he was not a very good student and could not get a scholarship to go to Oxford, and his family could not afford to send him—his father was a minor civil servant—without a scholarship. The father said, "You're going to join me in the India civil service," which was its own branch of the civil service in the English Empire, and [Eric] joined the police force. No one was more unsuited to be a bureaucrat or a policeman than George Orwell (the name he took), and he found it miserable and, after a few years, resigned.

But he did leave behind a brilliant essay, called "Shooting an Elephant," about the utter stupidity that bureaucrats get into once they've undertaken a task and the cruel things they have to do even though they know they are wrong. He had this deep suspicion of bureaucracy. What he wanted to be was a novelist; trouble is, nobody wanted to publish his stuff and nobody, in fact, would even be his literary agent. He became down and out in London and Paris; in one of his books, he described being very poor, simply living as a tramp. Then came the Spanish Civil War—1936 it broke out—when Orwell was at that very, very important age of his mid-30s; he was 33. To Orwell, the Spanish Civil War was the embodiment of the struggle that had been going on all through the 20th century between the forces of good and the forces of totalitarian government.

Up until this time, like many intellectuals in England—like many intellectuals in this country and other countries in Europe, as well—Orwell had blinders on about the true nature of the Soviet government. The Soviet government began in 1917–1918 in a great burst of hope. All through the 19th century, socialist thinkers had debated this question of how to get rid of private property. There had been many literally utopian schemes, such as setting up communities where everything was held in common.

But Karl Marx—who died in 1883—had written his great book *Das Kapital* to prove not only that private property was wrong but that, scientifically, it must disappear. It was the force of economics, the force of science, the force of history that would determine the ultimate triumph of a communist state, in which all property was held in common by the workers, the productive classes. Instead of government being a conspiracy of the capitalists—the wealthy—to exploit the productive classes, the productive classes would hold all property in common, and the capitalist class would simply disappear. This developed—this communist view of Marx—the force of a religion. Again, it is hard for us at this stage of history to understand this, but it was fervently believed as a dogma. Marx's works became much like a bible with their scientific proof of the triumph of communism.

In 1917, this became reality. The Russian government of the tsars was one of the most incompetent governments in history as it entered World War I. It didn't even have the intelligence to realize that World War I would be disastrous to it—disasters on the military front, economic disasters—until finally, in March 1917, it just literally collapsed. With very little effort, the tsar was forced to abdicate, a social democratic government came into power, and Russia seemed to be on its way to developing a constitutional liberal government.

But this wasn't the right thing for the Bolsheviks, for the communists. They had waited for this chance, and they weren't going to see it thrown away by a few liberal politicians. In November of that same year, 1917, led by the great revolutionary figure of Lenin, the Bolsheviks seized power. They ruthlessly eliminated not only the followers of the tsar but their social democratic enemies just as well—all of those who wanted to stand around and debate and discuss and vote; all of that was nonsense. A small revolutionary clique seizes power, and then it pushes through what is for the good of the people.

The Soviet government not only rid itself of its internal enemies, [but] it fought off foreign interventionists as French, British, even American and Japanese forces tried to overthrow the Bolshevik government. By 1922, it had begun to emerge. The cost had been tremendous—millions had died—but communism seemed established in one country. All over the world—from China to the United States and including Britain—liberal intellectuals looked upon this as the dawning of the new age. Oh, they heard many rumors that terrible things had been done, but if they had to be done, then it was in the name of this much greater good.

In 1924, Lenin died, and the struggle began for his legacy between two figures: Joseph Stalin and Lev Trotsky. Trotsky seemed the obvious candidate. He was brilliant; he had established a distinguished military record during the revolution. He was an intellectual, but he learned how to lead the Red Armies to victory, and [he was] a powerful speaker. Stalin [was] a morose man, very few communication skills, we might say today, but a master of manipulating people.

Suddenly, by 1927, Stalin had very carefully consolidated all real power into his hands. Trotsky found himself, first, exiled to Siberia and, then, exiled to Mexico, where in 1940, he would be murdered. Stalin became absolute master of the Soviet Empire. Comrade Stalin: He was so modest in his taste but the most ruthless dictator in all of history. Perhaps as many as 20 million people would die to put his great projects into place: his great canals, his industrialization of Russia, the huge dams that had to be built for the ordinary worker. Vast gulags, or labor camps, filled up so these projects could be put in place, and an entire new generation was educated to be communist.

In 1941, invaded by Hitler, Stalin proved strong enough to win the Great Patriotic War. In August of 1945, Stalin stood at the absolute peak of his power. It was in that very month of August 1945 that George Orwell published his *Animal Farm*. "Since 1936," Orwell said, "everything that I have written has been dedicated to the exposition of the evils of totalitarianism. I have fused my art and my politics into one comprehensive whole to describe the evils of totalitarianism." In the Spanish Civil War, he had gone into the republican forces, thinking that he was fighting for freedom against the fascists and that Hitler was the greatest evil in the world. But there, he had learned about communism at firsthand, from the communist troops who fought on the side of the Spanish Republic. He had learned that Stalin and Hitler were simply sides of the same coin, both absolutely devoted only to power and that power seemed to be the only cohesive, stable, unchanging element in human history, the desire of one or a few to dominate others.

He penned *Animal Farm* about all the brave hopes that had been raised with the abolition of private property or, in this case, the tyranny of man. After all, isn't man the greatest tyrant on Earth? Doesn't he exploit and kill, by the millions, little animals every day? We read Isaac Singer, didn't we, *The Penitent*? Singer told us that everyone who eats animal flesh is evil; a Nazi, he called them. The slaughter of the animals, the exploitation of animals by humans—to Orwell, this became the mechanism to describe [a] deeper question: Will human nature ever change, and what difference does private or public property make?

The story begins at a farm, Manor Farm, in England, and all the animals have come together one evening in March. They've had to surreptitiously come. Mr. Jones is the owner of the farm; he's just a simple farmer. He drinks a lot, he doesn't pay a lot of attention to his farm, he likes to sleep on the sofa, having had several beers and with a newspaper over his face. That night, he has fallen asleep drunk as well, so the animals are able to get out of their pens, and they come into the big barn.

The pigs arrive and all sit on the front row; the hens all come in; the cows come in. Various horses come in, like the strong workhorse Boxer, and Molly, the little horse who pulls the wagon, with her gay ribbons in her hair, looking for sugar the way she always does. The dogs bring in their little pups with them. And they all listen to old Major speak. Major is a 12-year-old pig, with great, huge tusks, and he knows the end is coming for him. But before he dies, he wants to tell his fellow animals about a dream he had, a vision. In that vision, he said:

"I saw Manor Farm taken over by us, by the animals. We drove out Mr. Jones. We established our own animal paradise. We all worked together. I see your eyes glazing over; you are little bored, aren't you there, Molly, thinking about whether or not you are going to get some sugar today? But listen to me. Have any of you ever pondered how exploitive humans are? We work all day for them, and they feed us just enough to keep us alive. They give us a little treat—like some sugar for you, Molly—and you're so happy you'll just keep on working. Yet where would they be without us?

"We're just as smart as humans, if you lock at it. We have all the skills that they lack. The only skill they have is being able to manipulate us. If we got rid of humans—if we all work together—then there'd be a paradise. You hens: How many eggs did each of you lay last week? How many of them have you seen? They've all been taken away. What happens to those little chicks that you will never see? The puppies that you have, they'll be sold; you'll never see them again. How many cows give milk on this farm, and how much milk is returned to them? It's all exploitation. I want you to join me in singing a song. It came to me in this vision. [Orwell describes it as being a little bit like "La Cucaracha" and a little bit like "My Darling Clementine," but something along the lines]: 'Beasts of England, beasts of Ireland, beasts of every land and clime, hear the joyful tidings of the coming golden time. Soon or later, the day is coming, Tyrant Man shall be overthrown, and the fruitful fields of England shall be trod by beasts alone.' [Old Major continues:] There came to me our flag. It's a green flag with a hoof and a horn painted in the corner; the hoof and horn entwined. I hope you will one day live to see that."

Old Major died not long after that, but the animals continued to dream his vision. The pigs—they were smart; they began to develop a whole doctrine called Animalism, which scientifically proved that animals were smarter than humans, scientifically proved that sooner or later, the human order would collapse, that animals would establish a great cooperative state, and all over the world, there would be Animalism. They began to work and labor for this great coming. They even developed their own doctrine—their own commandments—which they planned to write, as soon as they learned how to write, on the walls of their great barn: "What goes on two legs is an enemy. What goes on four legs or with wings is a friend. No animal shall drink alcohol; no animal shall sleep in a bed; no animal shall wear clothes; no animal shall kill another animal; and all animals are equal"—the commandments.

Then, on a midsummer's night eve, Mr. Jones went to the pub—the Red Lion—drank too much, came home, and fell asleep. All that day long, none of the animals had been fed. The cows had not been milked; they kept mooing and mooing and kicking their stalls, hoping somebody would come and feed them. But the workmen had all taken the day off, and Mr. Jones had gone off, and nobody came to take care of them. Finally, just as in 1917 starving workers and peasants rioted, so on this midsummer's eve, the animals rioted. They kicked down their stalls and they stormed toward the house. Mr. Jones heard them and he got the workmen, and they came out with their brutal whips to beat the animals back into their stalls. But this time, the animals would not take it, and they kicked and fought and drove. Mr. Jones fled; his workmen fled as the great Boxer, the mighty stallion, kicked them with his hooves, and the pigs butted them, and even the sheep butted them. The geese ran and bit their legs. Even Mrs. Jones fled, just like the tsar tried to do, throwing a few of her clothes in a carpetbag and rushing out the door. Suddenly, the animals owned the farm. How did it happen?

They went into the house, and they were amazed at all the luxuries that their work had bought. Picture the workers wandering through the winter palace in St. Petersburg with all the magnificent rooms and furnishings; so the animals walked and saw all of these glorious trappings that they had won. They met finally, and there in the barn, they proclaimed "Animal Farm"; no longer was it to be Manor Farm, but it was to be Animal Farm. They sang the song "The Beast of England" and raised their green flag.

Just as the European powers had thought something bad had happened in Russia but didn't feel strong enough to overthrow it, so all the neighboring farmers said, "This is terrible. Mr. Jones was run out, but he's a drunk, and the animals have control of it. But they can't last very long; they'll collapse," the same way that the European powers thought the Soviet Union would collapse. They just waited for the animals to collapse on their own. But they didn't. They worked together, and they had more to eat than they ever had before. [From] the milk, the little cows got strong; the little chicks were all raised. The only little troubling thing is that the puppies had disappeared; nobody could find the puppies. But nobody worried about that much, because they not only had cooperation and animal-hood, but they had the leadership of the pigs. The pigs outdid any other animal in their hard work and devotion to the cause of Animalism, particularly two pigs, Napoleon and Snowball.

Snowball was a wonderful speaker, and the animals found that they could all speak and communicate, and they very quickly taught themselves to write. In the old tsarist days, it was thought that peasants could never learn to write. In fact, one of the first things the Soviet Union did was to teach everybody to write, make everybody literate, so they could follow all the rules All the animals become literate. They proudly write their commandments up on the barn wall. They work together, and Napoleon and Snowball lead them. Snowball makes wonderful speeches and is very active in creating committees. Every animal is on three or four committees; everything from the amount of milk production—all of this is solved by committees and discussions. Every issue is freely debated. Napoleon just does what he's told and keeps kind of quiet.

Then, one day, the foreign interventionists come. It has become clear that Animal Farm is not going to collapse, and so the local farmers come, armed, in some cases, with guns and led by Mr. Jones, to recapture his farm. They can't allow this example to continue. They storm in and [launch] what becomes known as the Battle of the Cowshed. The animals attack, Snowball leading them, and they storm right into the face of shotgun fire. Snowball himself is wounded in the head; great Boxer rises up and smashes the men and drives them out. The animals win; the losses are heavy—one sheep is killed—but they have conquered.

From this time on would the other farmers just leave the animals alone; they know they can't take it back. Mr. Jones becomes a kind of vagabond, wandering around. To celebrate this great victory, medallions are issued: Hero of the Animals First Class, Hero of the Animals Second Class. The sheep is buried with great ceremony, and old Major is dug up and his head enshrined on a pole, the way Lenin is on view there in Red Square, as the founder of this great revolution.

They continue to work and to toil and to work and to toil. Then, one day, at one of their committee meetings, Snowball brings forth the idea, "Do you know how we could cut our workday?"

"No, how?"

"We could build a windmill."

"A windmill?"

"And generate electricity here at Animal Farm; we'd have all these labor-saving devices."

"A windmill."

Napoleon doesn't say much about it. He's asked, and he says, "I don't think a windmill will work. I think it will be a misuse of our resources at the moment."

But Snowball draws up these huge plans, and they get all ready to build it. Then the day comes to make the final decision. Snowball makes a wonderful speech—all the animals are ready to vote yes—when suddenly, Napoleon reappears, bringing with him—remember the little puppies? He has raised them himself, nine of them, into huge mastiffs with great collars around them, fierce, evil, and vicious. He doesn't say a word; he just unleashes them on Snowball. Snowball, in fear of his life, rushes out of the farm. Napoleon says, "Now, I don't think we need any more debates about anything."

But three weeks later, a new meeting is called, and Napoleon announces through his little aide, Squealer the Pig, that he has always thought it was a good idea to build the windmill. Snowball was opposed to building the windmill, but Napoleon is in favor. Just as in the old Soviet Union, history is immediately rewritten and everybody forgets what it was in the past. They begin to build this great windmill, and they have it raised, and all the farmers come from a distance: "Look at these animals that built a windmill!"

Then one night, it collapses, and Napoleon comes out with his dogs, and all the animals walk around. Napoleon asks the question: "Why did this fall? Snowball, Snowball, Snowball has found collaborationists inside Animal Farm, and with these collaborationists and foreign interventionists—the other farmers—he has destroyed our windmill. We must find out who the collaborationists are."

Suddenly, creatures begin to step forward; several hens step forward and say, "We did it; we collaborated." The dogs are unleashed upon them and they are killed.

A pig says, "I did it," and the dogs are unleashed upon him and he is killed.

Do you remember the trials of Stalin and all of these collaborationists with the Germans and Trotskyites who are found, because Trotsky was causing all this evil from exile? So, too, they're there on Animal Farm. One of them dares say, "But I thought one of our commandments read, 'No animal shall kill another animal.'"

"You didn't read it right, comrade: 'No animal shall kill another animal without due cause.'" The dogs are unleashed again. Napoleon has solidified his power.

Now he brings another plan before the animals: "Whoever said that we should not work with humans? Humans are our friends."

"But the commandment … [dog growling] Yes, yes, yes, but we thought all things with two legs are bad."

"No, no, no, no, no, you didn't read it right."

So he develops this huge scheme to have capitalism on Animal Farm, and all the eggs will be produced, the milk will be sold to these humans. Suddenly, Animal Farm finds itself getting very wealthy in terms of money, but the animals now have less to eat than they did under Mr. Jones. "Where's all this money going?" they wonder.

That's about the time that Napoleon and his pig friends move into the house and begin to sleep in the beds. Again, there are some brave animals who ask and say, "But I thought our commandment was 'No animals shall sleep in a bed'?"

"No, you didn't read it properly, comrade: 'No animal shall sleep in a bed with sheets.' But we pigs have to work so hard that we need to sleep in beds; how else could we come up with committees for you to work on?"

All through this, brave Boxer, the stallion, remains the most committed, intelligent follower. "If Napoleon says something is right, then it is right. Comrade Napoleon is always right."

The sheep are easy; anytime anybody has a dissenting thought, the sheep just start blathering: "Two legs bad, four legs good; two legs bad, four legs good," until they shout down any dissent. They can go on for hours. Napoleon now has all power in his hands.

But old Boxer is getting sick, worn out, hurt in one more attempt by the foreign interventionists—the other farmers—to take back the farm. He's getting very ill; his hoof is infected.

The little animals come to Napoleon and say, "What will you do with Boxer? We know what the evil Mr. Jones would have done. When a horse like that got ill, he would sell him to the glue factory."

"Oh, we will never do that; in fact, a hospital wagon is on the way."

The wagon shows up, and it has written on it "Glue Factory." A man gets out and pays Napoleon—who has now learned to walk on two legs and wear a little bowler hat—pays him money, and the animals have the courage to come up and say, "But are you selling Boxer to the glue factory?"

"Not at all. What you didn't understand is that [factory] is actually owned by a hospital now; they just haven't changed the sign yet." Boxer disappears.

"Can we bring him back for burial? He was the very hero of the revolution."

"No, his last words were to just let him rest where he was so no more expense will be made by the brave animals."

Then one night, large numbers of humans come to Animal Farm and they go in the house, and all the little animals crowd up and look into the window. There, they see all the pigs—the Pig Bureau—around the table. They are playing cards and drinking beer and cider that is made just for their own use there on the farm. They are playing cards and drinking with all these humans, with whom they're engaged in all these capitalist enterprises. They pass the cards around; there are some arguments over who's cheating or not. Then, one of the animals looks at one pig and he looks at a human, and he looks at one pig and he looks at a capitalist human, looks back and forth, and he can't tell any difference whatsoever. They look exactly alike. What has happened to Animal Farm?

They hear a voice boom out: "I have told you animals it is not Animal Farm. That was a false name; it was never called that." It is the voice of Napoleon. "It is and always shall be Manor Farm, and never do I want to hear 'The Beast of England' sung again. It is a revolutionary song, and we are a stable government doing trade and harm to no humans."

The rest of the little animals creep into the barn, and they look up at all their little commandments, how each one has now changed: "No animal shall drink alcohol in excess. No animal shall sleep in a bed with sheets." Then they look down, and there is only one commandment: "All animals are equal; only some animals are more equal than others."

Lecture Thirty-One
Josephus—*History of the Jewish War*

Scope:

The next five of our lectures on life lessons from the great books focus on the last theme: patriotism. Patriotism is the love of country. In the classical tradition, the duty we owe our country—our fatherland, as the Greeks and Rome termed it—far exceeds our duty to parents and family. Today, we study great books about patriotism because they make us better as individuals and better as citizens of a free country.

The story of the Jewish War was told by Flavius Josephus. He was a rabbi and general of the Jewish army. He survived and joined the side of the Romans, predicting the rise of the Emperor Vespasian. His history is a moving lesson in the love of freedom. Despite the peace and prosperity brought to the world by Roman rule, the Jewish people rose up out of love of freedom and duty to God. Despite the bravery of these Jewish freedom fighters, the Romans conquered. But they left behind the enduring lesson that to fight and die in the noble cause of freedom is never defeat. The story of the Jewish War is imprinted deeply in the politics of the contemporary Middle East.

Outline

I.   We turn now to the theme of patriotism. Patriotism is one of the most important themes to come to us through the great books tradition, yet today, we might ponder our own definition of patriotism and its relevance to our society.

II. The Founders of the United States looked for their great models of patriotism in history and, above all, in the history of the classical world. Patriotism in the age of the Athenian democracy was defined quite simply as the belief that the noblest thing one can do is to die for one's country.

  A. In his Funeral Oration, Pericles speaks about the young men who died in the first year of the war between Athens and Sparta. He speaks of the country for which they died and of a citizen's duty to make that ultimate sacrifice.

B. The Greek historian Polybius also spoke of the nobility of fighting for one's country when he explained how Rome had become absolute master of the world in one generation.

III. This same view is expressed by Flavius Josephus (37/38–100 A.D.) in his history of the great war between the Romans and the Jews, which for the Founders of the United States, took its place alongside Thucydides and Herodotus as a fundamental source of lessons for patriots in a new country and new world.

   A. Flavius Josephus was born Jewish and raised to be a Pharisee. He was carefully educated and became learned in the law.

   B. The Roman Emperor Augustus believed that limits should be set on the expansion of Rome and had refrained from annexing the territory of Judaea.

   C. Augustus faced a difficult decision when a group of leading citizens of Judaea asked that their land be formally annexed. He was reluctant, partly because Romans in general were perplexed by the complicated relationships of people in the Middle East.

   D. Augustus understood the potential for a Jewish revolt but also recognized the enormous strategic, economic, and military importance of Judaea. He saw that Judaea must be kept firmly in the Roman camp to prevent an Iranian invasion; thus, the decision for annexation was made.

   E. The Romans had great respect for the Jewish people, and the annexation treaty ensured basic recognition of Jewish traditions.

   F. The Middle East remained forever outside the comprehension of the Romans. They were baffled by the deep hatred between Greeks and Jews who, despite cultural intermingling, maintained a mutual sense of disrespect.

IV. In the period before 60 A.D., a number of Jewish prophets proclaimed the fall of Roman rule and the establishment of the kingdom of God. The Jews, it was said, must never have an earthly king; they must be a theocracy ruled by God directly. To the Romans, this was treason.

A. The idea that the kingdom of God had to be established through violence gave rise to a group of revolutionaries who considered themselves to be patriots.

B. These revolutionaries attacked Roman troops in an effort to force the Romans to react ferociously and immoderately, spurring an uprising among the Jewish people.

C. The failed policies of Emperor Nero and the power vacuum left in the wake of his overthrow fed the desire of many patriotic Jews to see their nation reestablished as a free power.

V. Josephus was at the heart of the revolution when it broke out. At 37 years of age, he was made a general and sent to Galilee to organize resistance against the Romans. There, he found himself in the midst of a civil war.

A. At about the same time, Rome found a capable general in Flavius Vespasian. He reduced large portions of Judaea and captured Josephus.

B. Imprisoned, Josephus told the Roman guards that he had had a vision in which he saw Flavius Vespasian as master of the world.

C. Vespasian told Josephus that he would be well rewarded if his prophecy came true.

D. When Vespasian eventually became emperor, he released Josephus, gave him a large stipend, and told him to write about the war.

E. In 70 A.D., the Roman general Titus undertook the suppression of the Jewish revolt by laying siege to Jerusalem.

F. Josephus writes in terrifying terms of the brutality and cruelty of war. On more than one occasion, he was sent by Titus to convince the Jewish freedom fighters to surrender, but they would not.

G. Jerusalem finally fell to Titus in 70 A.D., and he returned to Rome triumphantly with thousands of Jewish prisoners. Refusing to accept Vespasian as their lord, the Jews were brutally executed, and the Temple was destroyed.

VI. For one brave band of freedom fighters, the war was still not over. They took up their defense at the fortress of Masada. The Roman general and governor Flavius Silva was sent by Vespasian to lay siege to the fortress and put down the last of the rebellion.

A. The Jewish force at Masada was determined to fight to the death.

B. After a massive siege, it became clear to the freedom fighters that the fortress would be captured. Eleazar, the leader of the Jewish force, decided that the revolutionaries must die in freedom, along with their wives and children.

C. Before the Romans could enter the fortress, each Jewish father slew his own family and was, in turn, killed by one of 10 men chosen to carry out the last executions. The 10 remaining men then killed themselves.

D. Though the modern reader would consider the scene one of horror, the Romans saw it as a statement of absolute bravery.

VII. Troops enlisting in the Israeli army still take an oath of allegiance saluting these warriors for freedom. It is this same tradition—the Jewish people fighting and dying for their freedom—that led President Harry Truman to proclaim that America would always defend the brave nation of Israel.

Suggested Reading:

Josephus, *The Jewish War*.

Smallwood, *The Jews under Roman Rule*.

Questions to Consider:

1. Do you believe that by going over to the Romans, Josephus was a realist, a traitor, or a patriot?

2. What insight into the modern Middle East do you gain from studying *The Jewish War*?

Lecture Thirty-One—Transcript
Josephus—*History of the Jewish War*

We come now to Lecture Thirty-One in our exploration of the life lessons that we learn from the great books, and we turn to our theme of patriotism. Patriotism: It is one of the most important themes to come to us through the great books tradition. Yet today, we might ponder our definition of patriotism and how relevant many people find it to our own society. But for the great books tradition, the great books give us lessons not only for our lives as individuals but for our lives as citizens, and these lessons are all the more important if you are the citizen of a free republic.

And so it was that the Founders of our country looked for their great models of patriotism in history and, above all, in the history of the classical world. The Athenian democracy—the first democracy in history, the first government based upon the ideal of the greatest good for the greatest number of citizens—believed thoroughly that patriotism was the key to the survival of freedom. Patriotism was defined quite simply as the belief that the noblest thing you can do is to die for your country.

In his Funeral Oration, Pericles speaks about the young men who died in that first year—431—of the war between Athens and Sparta. He speaks of the country for which they died, of all the good things that country gives to its citizens, but of the ultimate duty of those citizens to fight for their country and to die for their country: "These men," he said, "each of them had his own hopes and aspirations, but when the moment of test came, they stood true in the line of battle, they died for their country, and they wrapped themselves in a mantle of glory that can never fade."

The Athenian view of patriotism was also captured by one of the epigrams written on those boys who had died for Athens and its far-flung wars of empire: "These are they who laid down their young lives beside the river Eurymedon; on land and on swift sailing ships alike, they fought with their spears against the foremost of the bow-bearing Persians. They are no more, but they have left behind the fairest memorial to their valor, the freedom of their native land."

So, too, in Rome, when the Greek historian Polybius wanted to explain to his fellow Greeks why in one generation Rome had become absolute master of the world—the fairly simple-seeming

Roman Republic triumphing over the great powers of Greece—it was, he said, "because the Romans are patriots and you no longer are. The Romans believe that the noblest thing they can do is to die for their country and the balanced constitution which gives them freedom, and you no longer believe that." In fact, we saw in our study of the plays of Menander how the Athenians in the 4th century had come to the belief that nothing was worth dying for, that they were much happier to live their lives as individuals, living the way they chose, not serving in the army, and not dying for their country. "The Romans believe in dying for their country," Polybius said, "and that is why they have triumphed. Moreover, they do not leave it to chance; they systematically educate young Romans to be patriots, to study the examples of the past and the heroic deeds that have gained Rome, first, its freedom and, then, its empire."

But the view that the noblest thing you can do is to die for your country is, of course, not limited to Greece and Rome; it was also true for one of the noblest stories of history: the ongoing struggle of the Jewish people for their freedom against Rome. It is told for us in the words of the historian Josephus—Flavius Josephus—and his history of the great war between the Romans and the Jews, which for the Founders of our country, took its place right alongside Thucydides, right alongside Herodotus as being a fundamental source of lessons for patriots in a new country in a new world.

Flavius Josephus was born Joseph, the son of Matthias. He was Jewish, but more than that, he was raised to be a Pharisee. He had been very carefully educated; he became very learned in the law, and for a brief period in his life, he lived in a monastery. He was one of the Essenes that we talked about when we discussed the Gospel of John. There, he shut himself off from the world, believing that the kingdom of God would come—brought about by the divine intervention of God himself—and restore the Jewish people to their greatness as a nation.

The Middle East: We are drawn back to it again and again and again. The headlines of today would have been comprehensible, in some sense, by Romans who read a newspaper—if such a thing existed— in Rome of the 1st century A.D. For in 6 A.D., Rome had found itself drawn into the annexation of Judaea. The Romans had, since the 2nd century B.C., been drawn tangentially into the Middle East, but in 6 A.D., the Emperor Augustus had a very difficult decision. He was absolute master of the world. He had brought his nation peace and prosperity. His empire stretched from what we would call France today all the way out to Syria, from the north seas of Germany to the sands of the Sahara. He also believed that limits must be set to the expansion of Rome, that Rome could not be, in today's terms, the policeman of the world. He had carefully refrained from annexing the territory of Judaea; Rome had occupied Syria since 63 B.C., but it had never annexed Judaea. But on this day, a deputation of leading citizens of Judaea had come to Augustus to ask that their land be formally annexed. Augustus was most unwilling.

Judea was very complicated; it was a cauldron of ancient hatreds. The Romans themselves were wise enough to know they did not understand the Middle East, and Judaea was particularly perplexing. It had large numbers of Greeks living there; towns like Caesarea were almost entirely Greek. On the other hand, the Jewish people were divided into a number of different groups, not so very different from Shiites and Sunnis today, in terms of it being incomprehensible to the Romans. There were those who were the Pharisees; there were the wealthy Sadducees, who focused their whole attention upon the worship of God and the Temple in Jerusalem; there were these Essenes, who withdrew from the world; there were also the Samaritans, and to a Roman, it was never quite clear how a Samaritan was different from a Jew. They both worshiped the same God, but they worshiped the God in different places, and the Jewish people did not regard Samaritans as Jews. It was all very, very complicated. [Augustus] also knew [that] the Jewish people, while they might want to be annexed to Rome on this day, would very quickly turn against him, and there would be very strong opposition to a Roman occupation of Judaea.

On the other hand, Judaea was of enormous strategic importance; in fact, it was the lynchpin in the entire Roman strategy for the Middle East. The Middle East was as important in relative terms to Rome as it is to the United States today. It was a source of an absolutely vital natural resource. Our society today functions on oil and, hence, the importance of the Middle East to us, but Rome functioned upon human power, and you have to feed humans. Italy had long since outgrown its ability to feed itself. Peace in the Roman Empire depended upon the ability of the Roman emperor to bring in large amounts of cheap grain and to keep the price of bread very, very low. Egypt was the source of three enormous crops of grain every year that fed Italy and other parts of the Roman Empire. To the east of Rome's dominion in the Middle East lay the land of Iran, the land of the Parthians, as the Romans called them. [It was] very well equipped technologically, superb military, with cavalry that could not be matched by the Romans.

Augustus, in 19 B.C., had reached a status quo with the Parthian, the Iranian Empire. They agreed to recognize each other's sphere of influence. But he knew that the slightest weakness on the part of the Romans would lead to an invasion of the Iranians, sweeping into Syria and sweeping through Judaea into Egypt, strangling the Roman Empire and its economic sources. Thus, Judaea had to be kept firmly in the Roman camp. So it was that Augustus made the decision to annex Judaea. In 6 A.D., in the words of the Gospel of Luke, "There went out a decree from Caesar Augustus that all the world was to be taxed, and this was the first taxation when Quirinius was governor of Syria"—pure history.

Pubilius Quirinius was a well-known Roman administrator; he was governor of Syria. Since Syria had long been part of the Roman Empire, he oversaw the annexation of Judaea and the first taxation, or what was, in fact, a census. The Romans tried to make every accommodation with Jewish religious sensibilities. In fact, Julius Caesar and Augustus both had great admiration for the Jewish people, and King Herod had been an important source of support for both Julius Caesar and Augustus. In fact, he had named one of his towns—Herod had—after Augustus and another of his towns after Julius Caesar. They had great respect for the Jewish people, and the annexation treaty provided certain basic recognition of Jewish traditions. For example, with connection to the Second Commandment, no graven images: Coins that circulated in Judaea did not have to carry the portrait of the emperor; they had no human portraiture whatsoever or animal portraiture. Secondly: The Roman soldiers generally carried battle standards which had a portrait of the emperor; in Judaea, the Roman troops that were stationed there had battle flags with no portrait of the emperor on them. Moreover, in recognition of the sacred status of Jerusalem, Augustus declared the city of Caesarea—a largely Greek city—to be the capital. That is where his procurator and governor would have residence, not in Jerusalem.

And so the annexation was carried out, and for years, the Romans did their best to accommodate Jewish feeling. In fact, the trial of Jesus—which would have occurred in 36 A.D. under Pontius Pilate—is an extremely interesting study in a Roman bureaucrat who was convinced that Jesus was innocent of the charges but knew he had to accommodate Jewish feeling and to respect the Jewish wishes in this matter. So, too, the travels of Paul around the Roman Empire—Paul, a Roman citizen—show again and again Roman governors trying to walk a careful line between accommodating Jewish feelings and also recognizing the rights of other citizens, like Paul, to speak [their] own minds given the freedom of speech that was an inherent right of a Roman citizen. Nonetheless, it was an impossible situation. The Middle East remained forever outside the real comprehension of the Romans. The deep hatred between Greeks and Jews baffled Romans.

Greek culture was all-pervasive in the Middle East: Many Jewish synagogues were built like Greek temples. Upper-class Jewish leaders had their children educated in Greek. The Old Testament had been translated into Greek. Greek philosophical terms permeated the study of the Old Testament, and one of the most influential intellectuals of the age—Philo, a Jew who lived in Alexandria—had written a series of works in trying to explain Judaism within the framework of Platonic philosophy. Despite all of the cultural intermingling, nonetheless, to the Jewish people, Greeks remained unclean, and to the Greeks, the Jews remained just wrong. There was no respect between them.

Roman soldiers were a constant source of trouble. They had a tendency to behave very arrogantly or, at times, very ignorantly toward Jewish traditions. Again and again, there would be riots, disturbances; the Romans would have to intervene with some force to put down a local revolt. There rose up among the Jewish people in the period before 60 A.D. a number of prophets proclaiming the fall of Roman rule and the establishment of the kingdom of God. The Jews must never have an earthly king; they must be a theocracy, ruled by God himself directly. To the Romans, this was treason.

The idea that the kingdom of God was not only going to be established but had to be brought into being through violence gave rise to a group of revolutionaries who considered themselves to be patriots, but whom the Romans believed to be terrorists. They were called the "Men of the Knife," the *Sicarii*. They would strike again and again in the streets of Jerusalem or other cities where Roman troops were garrisoned, kill a Roman soldier, stab him in the dark with a knife. [They] hoped by [this] series of assassinations and other acts of terrorism to force the Romans to intervene so ferociously, so immoderately that an uprising would occur spontaneously among the Jewish people. That is what they kept working for.

Into this volatile mix came the failed policies of the Emperor Nero. In 66 A.D., his heavy hand upon Judaea [and] the incompetent bureaucrats that he appointed to be governor led to a violent insurgency breaking out in Judaea. It was complicated by the fact that in 68 A.D., Nero himself was overthrown, committed suicide, and for one year—68 on into 69—there were four different claimants for the imperial power in Rome. In that power vacuum left by the disturbances in Rome, feeding upon this deep desire of many patriotic Jewish people to see their nation reestablished as a free power, celebrating the revolution as a revolution for freedom, the great and bloody civil war raged.

Josephus was at the very heart of this. When the revolution broke out in 66, he was made a general—37 years of age—and sent into Galilee to organize resistance to the Romans. There, Josephus describes, he found himself in the midst of what was, in fact, a civil war. The Jews were heavily opposed by Greeks. Terrible atrocities occurred in town after town: Greeks murdering Jews, Jews murdering Greeks. No quarter was asked, and none was given. Women and children were killed; in some cases, people were strangled with their own intestines as they waged this bloody civil war. The Romans intervened, but the Roman forces were highly distracted.

But in the midst of this, Rome found a most capable general, Flavius Vespasianus. Flavius Vespasianus reduced large portions of Judaea, and in 67 A.D., he captured Josephus. Josephus had been hiding in a cave with a number of other revolutionaries. They took an oath to kill themselves rather than to fall into Roman hands; they then drew lots as to who would kill the others, and Josephus was one of two chosen. They carried out the execution of their comrades. Then, when there were only two left, Josephus convinced his comrade not to kill him, and he wouldn't kill [his comrade], and they surrendered. Josephus escaped; he came as a Roman prisoner, was in his cell, and he kept telling his Roman guards, "I have had a vision about your general Flavius Vespasianus, and in that vision, I saw him as master of the world."

Word of this got to Vespasian, and he said, "I would like to see this prophet, for I understand that many prophets come out of Judaea."

Josephus was introduced to Vespasian, and said, "You will be the ruler of the world. Out of all this chaos and civil war, you will emerge and be emperor of the world."

Vespasian kept him in prison—treated him well, however—and said, "If this all comes true, I will reward you."

Ultimately, it did come true. Vespasian, following this prophecy—and also his sincere belief that he was the best man (and he was correct) to govern the Roman Empire—took his army back to Italy, won in civil war, and emerged as emperor of Rome in 69 A.D. He did not forget his friend Josephus: Josephus was released from prison, given a large stipend, and told to write about this war.

In the meantime, the war was continuing in all its violence. Vespasian appointed his son Titus to finish the war in Judaea and to do so by capturing the great holy city of Jerusalem. In the spring of 70 A.D., Titus—a capable general, strong administrator, a brave soldier himself, and absolutely ruthless on the field of battle—undertook to destroy the heart of the Jewish revolt and to put to an end forever—as he saw—to this goal of the Jews to be free and to govern themselves only under the dictates of God, to be a theocracy ruled over by their priests.

The city of Jerusalem—Josephus tells us, quoting census figures—had 2,700,000 inhabitants. It was one of the wonders of the ancient world, with massive fortifications that defied even the excellence of Roman siege techniques. But day by bloody day, Titus tightened the grip of the Romans around the city of Jerusalem. [He] cut off all food supplies, and inside the city, the brave freedom fighters began to starve. Starvation stalked the streets of Jerusalem, and the freedom fighters themselves were consumed by internal strife, struggles among one another, betrayals. Finally, the starvation grew so serious in the summer months that we are told parents even began to devour their children.

Josephus writes in terrifying terms of the brutality and cruelty of war and his conviction that the Jewish people had brought this upon themselves, that God willed them to be under the rule of Rome—as so many other nations were under the rule of Rome, God had willed that they be under the rule of Rome—and that God had chosen Vespasian to be master of the world. He looked upon the revolution itself—Josephus did—as wrong from the start, and on more than one occasion, the general Titus sent Josephus to the walls. He spoke to the Jewish freedom fighters within and said, "You must surrender." But they refused.

Finally, late in August, the city was fired, set on fire. Roman troops broke through using their catapults and battering rams, capturing the city, and then capturing the Temple itself. The last band of brave freedom fighters tried to hold out in the Temple itself, this most sacred of monuments, first erected by Solomon. But the fire swept in, hundreds died and then thousands, and a pitiful few surrendered. When this struggle was over, 1,100,000 had died of the Jewish people and 95,000 had been taken prisoner.

Titus came back to join his father in 70 A.D. in the most splendid triumph Rome had ever seen; thousands of Jewish prisoners led before him, these brave freedom fighters now in chains, still, however, refusing to admit any god except their God. They were tortured again and again by the Romans, and the demand was, "We will set you free if you will just swear that Vespasian is your lord."

"We have no lord but God," they said.

And so they were led in triumph and then brutally executed.

The Temple had been destroyed. For many Christians, this was a shockwave for Jesus himself had said the Temple would be destroyed within his own generation, and now it was. The sacred implements—the candelabra, the sacred tables—were all brought back to Rome, defiled by the hands of the Gentiles, and set up in the temple of Jupiter Optimus Maximus in Rome. The Temple was no more.

But for one brave band of 960 freedom fighters, the war was still not over. They took up their defense far out into the area around the Dead Sea at an enormous fortress: Masada. It originally had been built by Herod as a place of refuge. Rising up high out of the plain of the Dead Sea on a huge—what we would call—mesa, it circuited more than a mile, surrounded by mighty fortifications, [an] enormous palace inside it, with food of all kinds to last for years if a siege occurred, with vast stores of water. There, these 960 freedom fighters—the Romans called them terrorists, *Sicarii*; Josephus looked upon them as terrorists—but they were men who wanted freedom, and they brought their women and children with them. But Rome had one clear rule: They governed tolerantly as long as you followed them. If you ever crossed the Romans, there was no going back. They never set timetables to leave a country; they never drew down their troops. They waged war, once it had begun, to a complete finish, and in this case, it meant the destruction of the last element of resistance in all of Judaea.

The Roman general and governor Flavius Silva—picked by Vespasian and Titus for his cruelty, his ruthless attitude, and his military ability—began in 73 A.D. the siege of the fortress of Masada. It was a daunting task. There were only two pathways up, both of them strongly defended. One of them was called the snake. (You can still walk it today; it's a very moving experience.) It winds back and forth upon itself for several miles before it finally, in a very narrow gorge, arrives at the top of Masada. The other was a little easier but even more heavily defended by these Jewish freedom fighters, who had decided that was where they were going to fight and that was where they were going to die. Their only possibility of escape lay in inflicting so many casualties upon the Romans that they would leave them alone.

But it didn't happen. Flavius Silva built an enormous artificial mound just as high as Masada itself, making use of Jewish slave labor. Enormous catapults were brought up; battering rams were brought up; and day after day and night after night, the Romans hurled 300-pound stones with massive force into the walls of the city, the great fortress there, battering it and battering it and battering it.

They made a breach in the wall, and the Jewish defenders learned that they had to replace the masonry wall with a wall made of wood and earth. Once they had that in place, the Roman battering rams crashed against it but were so cushioned that the wall didn't collapse. So Silva gave the word to set a fire, and the wooden beams in the new wall began to burn savagely. The wind was blowing the flames back into the Romans' faces and they were about to abandon the siege, when suddenly, the wind turned, and it swept back into Masada and to the Jewish defenders. Josephus saw that, again, as divine retribution upon these terrorists who had begun the war.

It was clear the Romans were going to capture the city. That evening, the leader of the terrorists—of the freedom fighters—Eleazar, brought together his brave men. He told them there was only one solution for this: "We must all kill ourselves and our wives and children. We must die in freedom. We must let our women and children die in freedom, never to be touched by the Romans. What is death?" he said. "The soul lives forever. Life is our misfortune. Death is the greatest benefit God has given us. He is calling us to die."

They made their decision, and each father went to his wife and children and slew them there in the darkness of the night at Masada. Then the brave freedom fighters, the blood of their families still upon their hands, came together, and 10 of them were chosen. Each father then went back and lay beside his family, where they were dead; and his own throat was cut; and embracing his wife, he bled to death. Then the 10 freedom fighters that were left chose one to kill them. Nine were killed, and then the last one fell upon his sword.

The next morning, the Romans broke through with their battering rams, crumpling the wall. When they saw that scene—to us it might sound like horror—to the Romans, it was a statement of absolute bravery. They snapped to attention—the ordinary soldier did—and blew their trumpets in honor to these brave warriors.

Nothing ever goes away entirely in the Middle East. Still today, at Masada—this scene where freedom was deemed to be more worthy than life, where glory was chosen by these warriors who believed truly the noblest thing you can do is to die for your country—troops enlisting in the Israeli army still take the oath of allegiance as aircraft fly over, saluting these warriors for freedom. And it is this same tradition—the Jewish people fighting and dying again and again for their freedom and [the idea] that they must have a homeland—that led President Harry Truman, against almost all advice from his State Department, against the advice of General Marshall, his secretary of state, whom Truman admired so tremendously, to proclaim that Israel would be a new nation and that America would always be there to defend this brave nation.

Lecture Thirty-Two
Joseph Addison—*Cato*

Scope:

Joseph Addison's *Cato*, produced in 1713, was one of the most popular plays of its day, a favorite of George Washington and many of the patriots of the Revolution. *Cato* taught them and it still teaches us the patriotic lessons that shaped our Founding.

Joseph Addison was a man of letters, an essayist whose style won the praise of the critics of his day. He belonged to the Whig Party; admired the duke of Marlborough, the ancestor of Winston Churchill; and believed in constitutional liberty. His play *Cato* celebrated all these themes in the person of the Roman patriot Cato. Julius Caesar conquered the army of Cato, but he could not conquer Cato's love of liberty. Cato committed suicide rather than accept the terms proffered by the tyrant. Washington had this play performed during the winter at Valley Forge to inspire his troops with the lessons of freedom.

Outline

I. In this lecture, we continue our discussion of the theme of patriotism in the great books.

    A. Cicero believed that any free individual must also be a patriot, but he also believed that patriotism must be shaped by the four fundamental principles of wisdom, justice, courage, and moderation.

    B. Patriotism is the love of freedom and love of country and the willingness to die for one's country based on the assumption that its values and system of governance are right. The subjectivity inherent in that assumption frequently makes patriotism a difficult matter to decide.

    C. The Founders of our country were also faced with the question: What is patriotism? Had they been defeated, they would have been put to death as traitors under English law.

    D. We can find no sterner symbol of patriotism in the great books than Marcus Porcius Cato.

II. Cato understood Caesar's belief that he could revitalize Rome and preserve its empire. However, he also understood that the cost of such revitalization would be the loss of Roman liberty. Rome without liberty, no matter how grand its empire, would be nothing but an empty shell.

A. Cato, with few allies, fought Caesar every step of the way. He hated Caesar for his political and personal corruption.

B. Cato suspected Caesar of conspiring with those who wanted to overthrow the free republic.

C. By 48 B.C., it was clear that the people of Rome must make the choice between the liberty offered by Cato and the peace and prosperity promised by Caesar.

D. When the great civil war began, Cato cast his lot with Pompey. Defeated by Caesar at Pharsalus, Cato took his forces to Africa rather than seek amnesty from Caesar.

E. Although Caesar repeatedly defeated Cato's forces and offered him amnesty on generous terms, Cato ultimately chose death rather than accept Caesar's new order.

III. The U.S. Founders were inspired as much by Joseph Addison's (1672–1719) play *Cato* as they were by older accounts of Cato's life. Addison's *Cato* was one of the most influential literary and intellectual models for the American Revolution.

A. Addison was a deep believer in liberty. He had a distinguished career as a student of Oxford and had gained fame in Britain for his poem "The Campaign."

B. Addison's play *Cato* was first performed in London in 1713. It was meant as a warning to his fellow Whigs, as well as to the Tories, who supported a strong king and higher church.

C. The play is set in Utica, where Cato has already been defeated, and begins with his two sons, Marcus and Porcius. Both sons are in love with Lucia, the wife of Senator Lucius, but Porcius says they must put such matters aside and serve only their father and the cause of Rome.

D. Despite attempts by a number of important individuals to persuade Cato to reconcile with Caesar, Cato will not do so.

E. The Roman Sempronius attempts to steal away Cato's daughter and is killed. The Numidian prince Juba also wishes to marry Cato's daughter and is told that it is untimely to think of anything but freedom and liberty.

F. Cato learns that his son Marcus has been killed defending Rome; he vows never to disgrace his son's memory and never to agree to amnesty with Caesar.

G. Cato contemplates suicide despite the entreaties of his son Porcius to live and accept peace with Caesar.

H. In the final moments of the play, Cato drives his sword into himself. Before he dies, he permits Juba to marry his daughter and allows his son to marry Lucia. His body is carried to Caesar.

IV. The power of Addison's *Cato* is echoed in speeches by Patrick Henry and in the final words of such patriots as Nathan Hale. In 1777–1778, the patriot cause seemed almost on the verge of extinction. To raise moral at Valley Forge, George Washington organized a performance of his favorite play: *Cato*.

Suggested Reading:

Addison, *Cato: A Tragedy and Selected Essays.*

Fears, *Famous Romans*, Lecture Twelve.

Plutarch, *Life of Cato.*

Questions to Consider:

1. The Founders of our country admired Cato much more than Caesar. Today, it is the reverse. Why?

2. Cato was a Stoic like Seneca. Both believed in suicide before a compromise of fundamental principles. Do you agree?

Lecture Thirty-Two—Transcript
Joseph Addison—*Cato*

We come now Lecture Thirty-Two in exploring the life lessons that we learn from the great books, and we continue with our theme of patriotism. Patriotism is central to the very lessons of the great books tradition, but what is patriotism? Cicero believed that any free individual must also be a patriot, but he also believed—and discusses this in his *De officiis*, his book *On Moral Obligations*—that patriotism must be shaped by the four fundamental principles by which Socrates and Cicero both said we must live our lives: wisdom, justice, courage, and moderation.

Wisdom: Wisdom is knowing what is good patriotism; knowing that you are fighting for the right cause and that will, thus, be a cause of justice; that no unjust war can ever bring forth true patriotism. But what is an unjust war? There again, the classical tradition defines it quite clearly: It is a war in which you have been attacked, it is a war in which your ally has been attacked, or a war that you fight to remove an evil, tyrannical king. Cicero is proud that the Roman people always fought just wars, and he said that is why they always triumphed. Courage: Unless you are fighting for justice, courage is nothing but ferocity and bestiality. Moderation: You wage war with regard to rules, and even the enemy has certain rights and privileges if taken as a prisoner of war. Wisdom, justice, courage, and moderation all must be present to define patriotism.

We would wonder: Let's say the SS soldiers in World War II, were they truly courageous? Were they truly patriots if they were fighting for a cause—the Nazis—that any wisdom told you was evil, that had no justice behind it, and was absolutely without moderation or consideration? Patriotism is the love of freedom, love of your country, the willingness to die for your country, but based on the assumption that your country is right. That frequently makes patriotism a difficult matter to decide, because one person's patriot may be another person's terrorist. The Roman soldiers who fought against the Jewish freedom fighters and Josephus himself believed that the freedom fighters were engaged in an unjust war; that these freedom fighters themselves were a tyrannical government oppressing their fellow Jews; and that Rome had undertaken, at divine behest, their conquest. On the other hand, the Jewish freedom fighters believed that to accept the rule of Rome was evil, that they should worship only God and have only God as their king, that any actions they had to take were necessary to win this war.

The Founders of our country were also faced with this question of what is patriotism. After all, they were subjects of the British king, and in 1763, they had declared themselves *proud* subjects of the British Empire. Yet 13 years later, in the name of a higher law, they declared their independence from Britain. Had they been defeated, every one of them, under English law, would have been justifiably put to death as a traitor: drawn and quartered, hanged by the neck until they were almost dead, stretched upon the rack until their bones came loose from their joints, disemboweled while they were still alive and their intestines shown to them and then burned. In making this momentous decision, they looked back to Greece and Rome. Those were fundamental models for the Founders of our country. The fact that you fought a brave action and maybe lost in the name of freedom was no disgrace. They looked back to the Spartans, and more than one Founder hoped America would become a Christian Sparta, where the 300 Spartans who, laughing in the face of death, died at the hands of a vast army of Persians. They thought about the Athenians after the Battle of Salamis—their city lying in ruins, offered by the Persian king a most generous behest that Athens would be allowed to rebuild its city. The Persian king would pay all expenses, give every Athenian enough money to make him wealthy, and allow Athens to join the Persian king as allies, not as subjects, if only they would sign a treaty with him. And the Athenians announced, "Tell the king of Persia that as long as the Sun moves across the sky, the men of Athens will fight him."

One man in the assembly raised his hand and said, "Don't you think we should at least discuss this?" and the women and children of the Athenians went to the house of that man and stoned to death his wife and children, lest any family dissent.

These were the stern examples that stood before the Founders of our country, and there was no more stern example [of the attitude] that if you fight and die for freedom, you are always a patriot, even if you lose, than Marcus Porcius Cato. He was the single greatest role model for the Founders of our country, this somber Roman, slightly younger than Caesar.

At a time, let's say in the 60s B.C., as Plutarch—whose *Lives* was so influential for our Founders—tells the story: In the 60s B.C., most wise figures in Rome looked upon Julius Caesar as just one more cheap politician who'd do anything to win a few votes. From the outset, Cato recognized Caesar as the embodiment of evil. He understood the genius of Caesar; he understood the vision of Caesar; he understood Caesar's belief that he could revitalize Rome and preserve its empire. But he knew—Cato did—that the cost of such revitalization would be the loss of Roman liberty, and Rome without liberty, no matter how grand its empire, would be nothing but an empty shell. And so Cato, with very few allies, fought Caesar at every step of the way. It was said by Plutarch that much in Cato was like a sword that had not been tempered properly: It could not bend; it could only break. For Cato, the idea that politics is the art of compromise was a filthy lie; politics existed only in the truth and the lie, the right and the wrong. There are absolute rights and absolute wrongs, and he had set himself the moral compass of the liberty of Rome at every cost.

He hated Caesar for Caesar's personal corruption, as well. He looked upon Caesar as a drunkard and womanizer, and somehow, in every debate in the Senate—for both Caesar and Cato were senators—Caesar got the best of him. On one occasion, for example, a very serious situation had arisen—Rome was on the brink of civil war; Cato suspected Caesar of conspiring with those who wanted to overthrow the free republic (this was in 63 B.C.)—a messenger came rushing into the Senate house and gave a note to Caesar. Caesar was making a speech at the time, and he looked down at the note and then continued with his speech, and Cato said, "Read that."

Caesar said, "No, it's just a personal note."

Cato said, "Is it a note from the conspirators. You're engaged in a conspiracy against the freedom of Rome, as you always are."

Caesar said, "No, it's really not. It's just a personal note."

Cato said, "I demand you read it."

Caesar said, "All right, I'll read it. 'Dear Caesar, I cannot wait to find your arms around me. My lips hunger for you. I am expecting you.' Oh, and look, Cato, it's signed by your sister, Servilia."

Cato grabbed it, wadded it up, and threw it at Caesar. "You drunkard," he said.

But Caesar was more than a drunkard and a womanizer, and by 48 B.C., it was clear that Rome must make the choice between the liberty that Cato offered and the peace, prosperity, and freedom to live as you choose without any obligations that Caesar offered to the Roman people. There were still enough true Romans, as Cato saw them, to raise the banner of war against Caesar, and so the great civil war began in 48 B.C.

Pompey [was] no better than Caesar, Cato believed, but at least a useful tool to fight against Caesar. Cato cast his lot with the armies of Pompey as they fought for the freedom of the republic against Caesar, and defeat came at Pharsalus in 48 B.C. But Cato did not give up. Many sought amnesty from Caesar, including Brutus and Cassius, the later conspirators, but not Marcus Porcius Cato. He took his forces and went to Africa and there formed his own little Senate, his own little Roman Republic, and waited for the inevitable arrival of Caesar, there in Utica, not far from where Carthage had once been.

There Caesar came, and once again, the forces of Cato were defeated by Caesar. In 46 B.C. at the Battle of Thapsus, Caesar triumphed again and offered Cato an amnesty; offered Cato an important role in the new government, the new order, that Caesar would bring in; offered Cato whatever he wanted, just accept my hand in friendship and let us all work together as Romans. But can you ever make an alliance with evil? Cato withdrew into the city of Utica with just a few senators still around him and a small armed force. Again and again, even his best friends, even his own sons who were there with him—Marcus and Porcius—begged Cato, "Make an agreement with Caesar." In the end, he chose death rather than accept the new order of Caesar and died a martyr to freedom.

This model for the Founders—of Cato—[came] down through Plutarch's *Life* from the poem the *Pharsalia*, written by Lucan, the nephew of Seneca that we [mentioned] in the first of our lectures. [Cato] became a model for the Founders that death is a far more noble choice than servitude. But they found their inspiration as much in the 1713 play of Joseph Addison as they did in Plutarch, and Addison's *Cato*, now all but forgotten by us, was one of the most influential, literary, and intellectual models for our American Revolution.

Addison was a deep believer in liberty. He had had a very distinguished career as a student of Oxford, and then in 1704, he had come to British fame—known all over England—for his magnificent poem called "The Campaign," celebrating the campaign of the duke of Marlborough, John Churchill (Churchill's famous ancestor), that had resulted in the victory at Blenheim that made Britain into a continental power. Addison was a thoroughgoing Whig and a thoroughgoing believer in the Whig liberty. You'll recall that in 1688, the British—the English—and Parliament had driven out King James II. In 1649, the Parliament had beheaded King Charles. They had a brief period as a republic from 1649–1660 under Oliver Cromwell and briefly under his son. But they tired of this Puritan dictatorship, and they wanted all the frivolity of monarchy back, and they brought back, first, King Charles, but just like his father before him, he was very intent upon Catholicism.

We're tolerant, but the English Protestants were not, and Parliament was not. They did not want a Catholic king, and they did not want all the trappings of papal religion; they did not want the interference of the pope. In 1688, James II, the son, who seemed destined to raise his own son as a Catholic, was driven out of England. Parliament offered the throne to Mary, who was the daughter of King James, a Protestant—she turned against her father at the right moment—and her husband, ruler in Holland, William. William and Mary came to England and swore to a Declaration of Rights embodying fundamental principles, like the right of trial by jury. This was the Glorious Revolution, one without any real bloodshed and in which the principle of liberal parliamentary government was established. The Whigs had been those who were willing—the political party—to overthrow a king in the name of the true principle of liberty, including freedom of trade, traditional English liberties, civil and legal liberties, but also the bolder liberties of freedom of expression and freedom of speech. John [Churchill], the duke of Marlborough, also represented this Whig ideal of freedom and carried the banners of England far to the banks of the Danube.

In his 1704 poem, "The Campaign," Addison celebrated the great victories of Marlborough; received a very large stipend from the government, which was favorably disposed to his political views; and along with his old friend Richard Steele, established a series of magazines—*The Tatler*, *The Spectator*—and wrote for them a number of essays. Later on, English authors like [Thomas] Macaulay would say that if you wanted to develop a pure English style, you should study the essays of Joseph Addison. They covered a range of topics, literary but also political, always making the central point that true creativity and good government can flow only from true liberty from a limited government.

In 1713, Addison wrote his play *Cato*. It was first performed in London on April 13, 1713. April 13—as a good Classicist would know and Addison knew—was the feast day in ancient Rome of the goddess Libertas, the goddess of liberty. The Romans worshiped liberty as a divine being that they wanted to make part of their very commonwealth. So April 13 was the feast day of liberty, and Addison put on *Cato* in celebration of liberty. It was also meant as a warning, both to his fellow Whigs, as well as to the other party, the Tories, those who supported a strong king and a higher church. Queen Anne was coming to her end—she would die the next year, 1714—she had no children, and the worst thing they could do was to plunge England again into civil war. They must follow the Act of Succession that had been created by Parliament and offer the throne to King George, who would become King George as the closest Protestant, male relative. Let's avoid at all cost civil war, but only if we do not give up our liberty.

The play was a huge success. It played night after night after night on both sides of the Atlantic and the English colonies, as well; it became an enormous success, and Whigs and Tories alike celebrated it. Even Voltaire said, "Addison is the first Englishman to have written a real tragedy." By that, he meant a tragedy based on Aristotle's rules in the *Poetics*, including the fact that the whole of the tragic action has to occur in just one day. Remember how we talked about plays like *Macbeth*? They go over a number of days, long periods—*Anthony and Cleopatra* even over years—but all of this action occurs in one day.

It is all set in Utica, where Cato has already been defeated. Caesar is marching upon the little walled city of Utica; Cato has only his small number of senators and a few troops with him, as well as the loyal troops of the Numidian prince—the prince of North Africa—Juba, who is devoted to the ideals of Cato. There, he awaits the arrival of Caesar.

The play begins with the two sons—Marcus and Porcius—of Marcus Porcius Cato, men in their 20s, and they are both true to their father and both begin by debating what this day will bring: "For the day is dawning"—the day big with meaning for Rome and for Cato—"for the very question of liberty must be decided today. Our father will make only one decision, and that is that liberty is preferable even to death. Our father is the very model of Roman virtue and patriotism. His whole life is devoted to the ideal of absolute right, and in defense of that ideal of absolute right, he will lay down his life."

"Oh, I agree with you," says Marcus to his brother, Porcius, "but I find it so hard to concentrate."

"My brother, you're not still allowing your heart to sway you?"

"I am, brother," says Marcus, "I'm just so much in love with Lucia."

"How can you allow personal passions at this moment to sway you?"

But all through this play, Addison weaves a story of love and a story of patriotism. Because after all, is patriotism not just the love of country? A pure love is part of the purity of a moral code.

Marcus is deeply in love with Lucia, the wife of the senator Lucius, one of the true senators to Cato. He turns to his brother and says, "Porcius, you've got to go and plead my case to her."

Porcius is a little reluctant; he doesn't tell his brother, but he actually loves Lucia himself. But he says, "We must put all of this aside and serve only our father and the cause of Rome."

Next scene: In comes the senator Lucius; in comes Sempronius. Sempronius is a Roman, but all through the play, Sempronius has the goal of letting us know that sometimes those who speak most loudly in praise of patriotism are the most treacherous. He is determined to come to an agreement with Caesar and betray the cause of Cato. But he begins with a loud, boisterous speech: "We must fight to the death against Caesar. We will never surrender. Even if Cato weakens, I will fight on." In fact, he's in the midst of a criminal conspiracy to betray Utica to Caesar.

Then, in the next scene comes in the young Prince Juba, and he's accompanied by his old adviser, Syphax; both of these are Numidians. The king of Numidia has fought on the side of Cato, and Juba wants to convince Cato to leave Utica and follow him into the wilds of Africa and continue a guerilla campaign. But wily old Syphax, his adviser, begins to try to lure Juba down the path. He says to young Juba, "Have I not marked that you're in love with Marcia, the daughter of Cato?"

"Yes, yes, I am. I love her so much. I love her because she's like her father, stern in her virtues."

"Do you think her father will ever allow her to marry an African like you?"

"Of course, he will."

"Will he? Even if you have all the virtues, he will never think you the same as a Roman. Who are the Romans anyway? What makes them greater than we Numidians?"

"Leave me alone, Syphax. Where would you guide me?"

The next act opens with Cato coming onto the scene; it's our first sight of him. All around him are senators begging him to reconsider the offer of Caesar, to accept an amnesty of Caesar. "Never," he says. "The time has come for only one thing: chains or freedom, liberty or death. Damn Caesar for all his virtues and amnesty. Of course, he's a great man, and by that very greatness, he will destroy Rome."

The love plot thickens: It turns out that Sempronius is also deeply in love with Marcia, the daughter of Cato, and he tries to steal her away and is killed on the spot. Marcia's able to announce her deep love for the young Juba.

Juba goes to Cato and says, "Will you give me your daughter?"

Cato says, "I have told you before, this is not the time to think of anything but freedom and liberty."

Then terrible tidings are brought to Cato. His son Porcius rushes in and says, "My brother, Marcus, is no more. Traders were trying to flee outside the city walls, and Marcus stood before them with sword in hand and laid down his life."

"Did he die with all his wounds in front?" asked Cato.

"Yes."

"Then bring his body to me." Cato looks upon the corpse of his son with many a sword wound in it and announces, "I am satisfied. It is a pity that we have only one life to lay down for our country and the cause of its liberty. I will never disgrace my son. We will never agree to any amnesty with Caesar. I blame none of you who might want to go and kiss the hand of Caesar, but I will stay on here."

Juba comes up and says, "How your spirit inspires me like a comet. I, too, want to die for Rome and for freedom. You are the very model of virtue and patriotism, of honor, justice, courage, moderation, and of true wisdom."

"Yes," says Cato, "but where I go, I fear that no one can follow."

His son says, "Dad, you're not thinking of suicide?"

"That one way always lies open to us, doesn't it? When the world is proved so false to us, there's always the way of death. Did Socrates not ultimately choose death rather than dishonor?"

"Father, please don't talk that way."

"Leave me alone," says Cato as the evening dawns. "I wish to be alone with my books."

In the last act, there is Cato reading Plato's dialogue the *Phaedo*, on the immortality of the soul. "Yes," he says, "you have it right, Plato. Life is but the curse. We have been, all along, tied down with all the chains of our worldly possessions. How weary I am of all the falseness of the world. We have been preparing for death, and I understand that now, and with death, the soul is unleashed. It flies upward to God, and there, we'll always be at home." His son pokes his head into the room. "What are you doing here, Porcius? I said to leave me alone."

"I just came to get something, Dad."

"What is it?"

"Just this," and he grabs the sword out from under the pillow of Cato and rushes out the door.

"Come back with that sword! Come back!"

"No, Dad! Please!"

Cato takes the sword and lies back down, continues his reading. "Yes, yes. No, you're right, Plato. We can never prove that the soul is immortal; we only believe it. In that belief, it's a fair prize and a glorious hope that we will live forever." And so tranquil is he that he falls asleep; wakes up, refreshed; reaches under his pillow; and draws out his sword.

His son has brought word that they can escape by sea, as well as accept an amnesty from Caesar, but Cato has had enough of this treacherous world. In the final moments of the play, he drives his sword deep into his stomach. So carefully has Addison read his Plutarch that he even captures the final moment of Cato as the son rushes in and the daughter rushes in. Cato is lying there, still alive—he hasn't been able fully to kill himself with his sword—and he looks up to his daughter and says, "My dear, in the old days, this would not have been possible, but you marry Juba. He is worthy for a Roman, and together, both of you live, accept the new order. My death is enough of a sacrifice. You my son, Porcius, take Lucia as your wife. You, too, raise up a family; live in a new world; know no more of sadness."

"But you can join us in that new world, Father. It won't be the same without you."

"Caesar will never gloat over Cato." He reaches in—and he did this in real life—and with his hand, rips out his intestines and expires there on the floor.

"Let us carry the body of great Cato to Caesar; even in his death, he will protect us by his virtue."

How fully these lines became embodied in the Founders of our country is shown in speeches like that of Patrick Henry, there in the Virginia House of Burgesses. Trouble has already broken out in Boston, but wiser heads there in Virginia and Williamsburg had said, "There's no way we can take on the might of England. It will be like taking on the might of Rome, that vast empire. We must find a way to negotiate."

"Peace, peace?" says Patrick Henry. "Is peace so sweet, life so dear, it has to purchased at the price of chains and slavery? I know not what course others may take, but give me liberty or give me death."

Or, also quoting the lines of Cato, a young Connecticut schoolmaster—knowing his Latin well—Nathan Hale, taken prisoner by the British, goes to his death, as the British officer said, "like a gentleman." He has been caught as a spy and will die as a spy. But as he looks out over the crowd of British officers, he says to them, as did Cato, "I only regret that I have but one life to give for my country."

In 1777–1778, the patriot cause seemed almost on the verge of extinction. The army [was] trapped there at Valley Forge, starving day after day, morale sinking to its lowest point, and to revive that flickering morale, George Washington put on—there at Valley Forge—his favorite play. He didn't care much for the theater, but he loved *Cato*. There, [with] the officers acting out the parts, the men in their rags watched as Cato declaimed again, "This will not be the last Sun of liberty for Rome."

Lecture Thirty-Three
George Washington—Farewell Address

Scope:

George Washington's life and his Farewell Address teach us the deeper meaning of patriotism. Freedom was the bedrock of principle and the moral compass that guided Washington's life. As general and as president, he was the model of civic virtue and true patriotism. He subordinated his self-interests to the good of the country as a whole.

Washington's Farewell Address to his fellow countrymen, published in 1796, ranks with the Declaration of Independence, the Constitution, and Lincoln's Gettysburg Address as a fundamental testament of American freedom. His message should resonate and admonish us today. He tells us to put aside sectional and party division in the name of the unity of our country. Unity and our Constitution are the surest foundations of liberty. He warns us to be on guard against the encroachment of government power on freedom. He says that liberty rests on morality and religion and that fiscal responsibility is essential to government trust. Finally, Washington urges his fellow citizens to avoid foreign entanglements. Let us try to be friends with every nation but tied to none.

Outline

I. We continue our exploration of life lessons that we learn from great books with a focus on the ideal of patriotism. In this lecture, we turn to an individual who represents the very embodiment of patriotism from an American perspective: George Washington (1732–1799).

   A. In 1781, Washington received information that the French fleet had sailed from the West Indies and was approaching the bay off Yorktown, Virginia.

   B. Washington decided to quickly move the combined French and American troops to Yorktown to prevent the British fleet from arriving to supply British General Cornwallis.

   C. Cornwallis was cut off from supplies by sea when the French fleet triumphed over the British.

   D. Washington and his French allies began their formal siege of Yorktown, and Cornwallis was forced to surrender.

E. King George, hearing the news and facing a new British government, was forced to discontinue the war, ending the American Revolution.

II. Washington's achievement as a general was stunning. He created an army, found the funding for it, and devised a strategy to defeat the greatest empire of the day.

    A. As negotiations went on in Paris, the troops who had served Washington could not be dismissed and had not been paid for their service.

    B. Washington learned of a letter circulating among his officers that suggested he assume the position of king to prevent the collapse of the new country.

    C. Washington refused and promised the men that they would be paid. When the peace treaty was finally signed, Washington's men were paid, and the general surrendered his commission to the Continental Congress.

    D. The country was in danger of fragmenting. James Madison and others wrote to Washington asking him to take part in a convention to revise the Articles of Confederation.

    E. Washington repeatedly refused to return to public service, but he eventually acquiesced and traveled to Philadelphia to assume the chairmanship of the convention.

    F. Washington was unanimously elected president.

III. When Washington assumed the presidency, the country was bankrupt. The United States could not protect its frontiers from attacks by Native Americans or enforce the terms of the treaty with the British. Washington appointed a superb cabinet—another example of his intelligence—and, with his advisers, hammered out the future of the nation.

    A. The potential for power existed in the office of the presidency, but Washington made it a reality.

    B. An insurgency broke out in Pennsylvania, and Washington himself commanded the troops that put down the insurrection. Order was restored with no real bloodshed, and the authority of the federal government was made clear.

    C. Washington delegated authority to a trusted general to bring peace to the embattled Ohio Valley.

D. Alexander Hamilton skillfully organized the finances. His efforts were so successful that when the French Revolution broke out and investment opportunities in France dried up, Europeans began to pour money into the United States.

E. Washington delicately led the country between the dangers of intervention on the side of France or Britain when a war broke out between the two countries.

F. Many imagined that Washington would stay on for a third term as president, but he did not.

IV. On September 19, 1797, a letter from George Washington was published in the *Philadelphia American Daily Advertiser*. It is known today as Washington's Farewell Address.

A. Washington explained his reasons for returning to private life rather than staying on as president, pointing out that the country was now well established.

B. He boasted that the Constitution supported union, which was the country's strongest bond and the best foundation for freedom.

C. Washington pointed out that in guarding the Constitution, Americans must be aware of the encroachments of power.

D. He also advised Americans about the danger inherent in partisan strife.

E. Liberty, he said, must be guarded by morality and religion. He suggested that no nation will endure if it is immoral; it must have a moral citizen body that operates on the virtues of patriotism, frugality, honesty, and justice.

F. Finally, Washington advised against "foreign entanglements." He advocated commerce but with fiscal responsibility, and suggested that we should trade with other nations but avoid alliances.

V. Washington, recognized even by former foes as the greatest man of his day, retired to Mount Vernon. When he died, the ships of Britain and France, though they were poised to go into battle, both lowered their flags as a sign of respect for the passing of this great man.

Suggested Reading:

Ellis, *His Excellency, George Washington*.

Spalding and Garrity, *A Sacred Union of Citizens*.

Questions to Consider:

1. What portions of George Washington's advice are the most disregarded by us today?

2. Do you accept the judgment that George Washington is the greatest American?

Lecture Thirty-Three—Transcript
George Washington—Farewell Address

We come now to Lecture Thirty-Three in our exploration of the life lessons that we learn from the great books, with our focus in this final section on the ideal of patriotism. We want in our next three lectures to focus upon three individuals whom I believe represent the very embodiment of our ideal of patriotism from our American perspective: George Washington, George Patton, and Theodore Roosevelt.

But we begin with that greatest of all Americans: George Washington. I want you to put aside where you are at the moment and go back in time to August 1781, and we're in New York. Washington has just received dramatic information that the French fleet has sailed from the West Indies and, on a bold naval expedition, is coming up to the bay off of Yorktown, Virginia. Washington already knows that General Cornwallis has failed in his campaign in North and South Carolina and has retreated to Yorktown, hoping to be reinforced by the British fleet. So we have come a long way from our last lecture, when Washington was there at Valley Forge [with] his starving, freezing army, watching Cato and reviving their spirits by this story of Roman virtue. Now, it is an American virtue that is about to be put to the test. Washington, in consultation with his French ally, the Count de Rochambeau, decides to move the combined French and American troops southward from the New York area down to Yorktown and to do it rapidly enough to prevent the British fleet from arriving and supplying General Cornwallis.

On August 21, 15,000 troops—7,000 American, 8,000 veteran French troops—begin the march from New York to Yorktown. We should always remember that France was our first ally and that the military and financial aid of France was absolutely crucial to winning the Revolutionary War. But in the meantime, the British fleet must be stopped. On September 5–8, a tremendous naval battle is fought off of Yorktown, and for one of the very few times in the history of the British fleet, the British are defeated. The French fleet has triumphed, the British fleet is driven out of the waters, and the French set up a complete blockade by sea of Yorktown. Now, General Cornwallis with his British force is cut off from supplies by sea, and soon, they will be cut off from supplies by land.

On September 28, the British army sees the arrival of French and American troops under General Washington, and the Americans are then joined by 8,000 militiamen who have come from Virginia. It is roughly 23,000 American troops, along with their French allies, who begin the formal siege of Yorktown. Huge entrenchment lines are dug all around the fortress that the British have erected. The French are superb at setting up fortifications and siege lines. By the 9th of October, the British are in a desperate situation. The American and French cannons have been dragged up almost to point-blank range; they are firing time and time again into the British entrenchments. Finally, the last two British small redoubts—or little fortresses—on the perimeter of their lines are captured. Fort number 9, as it is called—or redoubt number 9—is captured by French troops who, making a quiet attack, a secret attack, carry only axes and overwhelm the British garrison. Then, redoubt number 10 is carried by Americans under the leadership of Alexander Hamilton. He's on the staff of Washington, but he has asked for special permission to carry out this raid.

And so it is that on October 17, the Americans see a young British drummer boy, resplendent in his scarlet coat, stand upon the ramparts and beat out the drum signal for parlay, "let's talk." Washington has only one set of terms for General Cornwallis: It will be unconditional surrender. We can still visit the small house where they carried out the negotiations. Cornwallis's agents are deeply distressed at the idea that they will surrender, not only unconditionally but without the honors of war. For the honors of war are all-important to the 18th-century ideal of gallantry, and that is, to say you surrender, but your men keep their weapons—they march out on their own word that they will not use these weapons again against you—and the surrendering force gets to play whatever tunes [they] choose. But generally, [they] will choose tunes that will celebrate the army that has won the battle

In this case, Washington is absolutely adamant. The point is made to Cornwallis: "You did not give honors of war to our men who surrendered at Charleston and Savannah, so why should we give honors of war to you?"

"Yes, but they were rebels."

"We're not rebels anymore, are we?"

The agent of Cornwallis says, "We will not get any better terms than this, my lord."

"All right." Cornwallis signs it but notes [that] His Majesty will be most annoyed.

King George *was* most annoyed when he learned of this surrender. He rushed into his wife's bedroom and shouted, "It is all lost." It was all lost: The government that had supported the war—the government of Lord North—collapsed. A new government came into power, and it was soon decreed that anyone who recommended [or] advised the king to continue this war against the American colonies should be regarded as a traitor. On October 19, with anger in their faces, the British troops marched out and surrendered, and the American Revolution was over.

George Washington is, in my view, the most successful American general. He had the hardest single task—to create an army, to find the funding for it, to find the strategy to lead it to victory—and he did all of this against the greatest empire of the day, the best army of the day (the British army), and the greatest fleet of the day (the British navy).

The war was won. But months went on—the peace negotiations continued in Paris—and the troops who had served Washington so loyally had not been paid. They were still kept under arms because until the peace treaty was actually signed, they couldn't dismiss the Continental Army. These men who had left their farms, left their families, fought in this long and desperate struggle against tremendous odds could not even get paid by the Continental Congress.

They were in Newburgh, New York, on the Hudson River on March 15, 1783; [they] still not been paid. Washington became aware that there in the camp, there was circulating a letter drawn up by anonymous officers. The letter suggested that Washington be approached and asked if he would become king or dictator because it was clear that this set of colonies—now states—would collapse. They turned to him, as so many armies in the past have—like Julius Caesar, as Napoleon would later—to become a dictator. Washington called his officers together. How many great generals in history can you imagine who would turn down this opportunity? But he called them together, he came out, and he began to try to read a response that he had written. But he couldn't read it. He had grown very farsighted, so he tried to pull out his glasses, and he couldn't get them out. He fiddled with them and fiddled with them and, finally, with an oath—because Washington never minded swearing—he said: "I have grown gray in my country's service and now I have grown blind. But let me just tell you this: Nothing in all my life has so wounded me as the very idea that some of you would imagine that I would want to be a king. I don't know how I'm going to get you paid, but I will get you and all the men paid. Now go back to your quarters."

And so they did. What a magisterial act. Finally, they were paid, the peace treaty was signed, [and] Washington surrendered his commission to the Continental Congress, now the Congress of the United States, and made his way back to Mount Vernon. That is all he wanted to do: to spend his last years with his beloved Martha.

Martha had come to him there at Valley Forge. Every morning during that cold and bitter winter, he would give his orders for the day, and then he and Martha would retire for one hour—just to be together—and you had better not dare disturb him during that time. Now, he had gone back with her, but duty called again. By 1787, the wise heads in Europe were absolutely convinced that the American experiment would fail. The country was bankrupt. In the fall of 1786, there had been a military insurgency in western Massachusetts, led by ordinary farmers who had been soldiers in the Revolution whose land was being taken away from them because they could not pay their debts because they themselves had been paid in worthless paper money. The country itself seemed in danger of fragmenting into various sections. Even on the frontiers of states like Georgia and North Carolina, the government could not offer protection to the settlers from savage attacks by Native Americans. Once again, the country turned to Washington. All through that winter of 1786, turning into 1787, James Madison and others wrote to Washington again and again asking that he take part in a convention to revise the Articles of Confederation. Such a convention had been called for Philadelphia for May of that year, 1787.

Washington again and again wrote back and said, "I have had enough of public service. I do not wish to be further involved in politics. I have gained a certain reputation among my fellow countrymen; I do not wish to see it destroyed in what I know will be a futile enterprise. Let me stay and take care of my finances and live out my years, as I wish to be a farmer."

But finally, duty was stronger, and he went to Philadelphia, assumed the chairmanship of the convention, and behind the scenes, played the most important single role in bringing about the Constitution. His moral authority again and again intervened, perhaps most significantly when there was a discussion of the executive power. Under the old Articles of Confederation, there was no executive whatsoever. All governmental business was done by committees, and there were some 99 committees operating in 1787. The convention was convinced that a strong executive power was needed. On the other hand, they worried about the concentration of power in the hands of a president who would be commander in chief of the armies; so many times in history that has turned into despotism.

But when it was put about that General Washington would agree to be the first president, then that removed all worries that anyone had. Isn't that moral authority—for a country to be willing to entrust its destinies to you because they know you will not abuse your power? The Constitution came into being, and the Constitution is but the embodiment of the patriotism of the ordinary American of the day. Yes, these 55 delegates drafted a Constitution, but it was ratified by the Americans as a whole, and Washington was unanimously elected by the electors as the first president.

I want you to ponder what Washington achieved as president. When he assumed office, the country was bankrupt. The United States had no credit whatsoever in Europe. The United States could not protect its frontiers from the Native Americans. The British were not following the regulations of the treaty. They had not abandoned forts like Detroit [for] the simple reason that the Americans were not fulfilling their part of the treaty by assuming the debts for British merchants. So [the country was] bankrupt and a laughingstock in Europe, with no army and no ability to raise income through taxes. When Washington stepped down, the credit of the United States was established on a firm basis that brought in large amounts of European investments. Our frontiers were secure. The British had followed all the regulations in the treaty itself, and this nation was on the path of progress and unity.

He appointed a superb cabinet. Washington is one of the examples of what makes a great man. You can tell a mediocrity who's in a position too important for him or her because they appoint people who are weak and yes-men, and they don't want anybody who can threaten them. Not Washington—he picked the brightest and most patriotic of his young fellow Americans: Alexander Hamilton, to take care of the treasury; Thomas Jefferson, to take care of the role of secretary of state; Henry Knox, who had become a superb officer of artillery from being a bookseller in Boston during the Revolution, appointed him secretary of war. They hammered out the future of this new nation.

There was potential power in the office of the presidency, but Washington made it a reality. An insurgency broke out in Pennsylvania. This was a real test case of whether the federal government had enough power to keep the states from splitting off. Washington had some sympathy with the men who raised up the insurrection. They were Revolutionary War veterans, and they were rising up, in their view, for the same reason that they had revolted against the British, that is to say, unfair taxes. They made whiskey. They grew corn, but corn wasn't much of a cash crop unless you turned it into whiskey, and whiskey was what they paid their taxes with. Whiskey was what they used as barter out on the frontier. Alexander Hamilton, as part of his attempt to raise taxes—raise enough currency to supply this new government—had put a tax on whiskey. They rose up against it. Although he had sympathy for them, Washington himself commanded the troops; 12,400 militiamen marched out, larger than almost any army that was assembled by the Americans during the Revolution, and put down this insurrection with no real bloodshed whatsoever. The authority of the federal government was made clear. The Ohio Valley, [which] had come into the new country as part of our settlement with Britain, seemed about to be an absolute failure because the Indian attacks of the Shawnees were so fierce that the settlers were almost afraid to go out there. Washington again found the right man—Anthony Wayne, trusted general from the time of Valley Forge, a bold general, so bold that his troops called him "Mad Anthony Wayne." He went out and, in the Battle of Fallen Timbers, defeated the Shawnee Confederation and made peaceful the whole area of the Ohio Valley. This was a federal government that could defend itself from outside attacks, as well as from internal insurrections.

Hamilton's arrangements of the finances of the new country were so superb that when the French Revolution came in 1789, Europeans, no longer able to invest in France, poured large amounts of money into this new country. All of this Washington achieved. At the same time, he delicately led this country between the dangers of intervening on the side of France—our traditional ally—or on the side of Britain when the war between Britain and France broke out as a result of the French Revolution. He took enormous criticism, but he steadfastly held the course.

Then came the great test. He had served two terms; he didn't want to serve that second term, but he had been convinced to do it by advisers. When the second term was nearing its end, once again, wise Europeans, who never really understood America, were absolutely convinced that Washington would stay on, alleging that the difficult foreign situation required him to remain as president. Many in the country not only thought it would happen, but they wanted it to happen.

So it was on September 19, 1796, there appeared in the *Philadelphia American Daily Advertiser*, a newspaper of Philadelphia, a letter from George Washington to his fellow Americans. We call it the Farewell Address. Can you imagine the hoopla that surrounds a president giving any address today? All the staged clapping, the walking into a room, the playing of triumphal marches; no, [there was] none of that. Just Washington writing his letter by hand, giving it to the newspaper editor, Mr. Claypool, and then going off to Mount Vernon for a vacation, so that he wouldn't be there to answer any questions, not holding some grand press conference. Of course, there were no news commentators to dissect Washington's Farewell Address.

This is what he wrote to his fellow Americans:

Many are now asking [he said] whether I will be a candidate for the upcoming elections, and I write to say no. I have served my country, and now it is time for you to turn our destinies over to a new president. This is as it should be. This is no reflection upon my deep gratitude to you, my fellow countrymen, for all the honors that you have bestowed upon me, and it is no shirking of my duty. Our country is now well established. We have a functioning Constitution that every day gives us ever more security for freedom. My personal wish to return to private life that I've held for so long, as well as my own sense of patriotism and my gratitude to you, all come together in this decision.

I might stop now, for I have told you why I will not run again, but I wish to go on as an affectionate friend would and give you some final advice. Because we have gone through so much together, I have such deep affection and gratitude to you, my fellow Americans, and I know the path of our nation is so unique that I want to admonish you. I need not admonish you about liberty; that is ingrained in every fiber of your being. We have fought a war for freedom, and we will never lose that freedom as long as we hold dear those ideals for which we have struggled. But at the heart of that freedom is our union, and the union is our best foundation for freedom. There will be those who put themselves forward as patriots, who will try to beguile you away from the union. Sectional differences do exist among us. But to all Americans, whether from the North or the South, the East or the West, I would hold up the fact that the union is our strongest bond. The commerce of the East flourishes because the South is the market by which its manufactured goods are bought. The South: [The] produce of its fields is taken up to the North. In growing terms, the produce of the West comes to the East, and as more canals are built, roads are built, the union will be made even stronger in terms of this commerce.

Our union is the dearest security for our freedom. There are sectional differences, but we are, above all, Americans, brought to be Americans by our common trials [and] our common triumphs, and that should be your proudest designation: I am an American. To support that union, there is the Constitution. This has come together out of the full flowering of the wisdom of this very age in which we live. It has been brought before the American people; it has been debated in the fullest and most public terms. I do believe that no single instrument of government has ever been devised that is more suited to guaranteeing true freedom. The Constitution, along with the union, is what makes us all Americans. And that is where your devotion must be: not to any single state, not to any single section, but to that union and to that Constitution.

In guarding that Constitution, you must ever be aware of the encroachments of power. The Constitution is a superb set of checks and balances, but it is in the very nature of power [Washington reminds his fellow citizens] that it will expand until it is checked by an opposite power. Whether it is the Congress, or whether it is the president, or whether it may be the judicial branch, each is a danger if it is allowed to grow too powerful. Beware of encroachments of power and [remember] that the very good government you enjoy rests upon your constant vigilance, for you are the true guardians, you, the ordinary American—not the politicians that you elect, but you, the ordinary Americans.

Union, Constitution, a vigilant citizen body, and yes, you must avoid parties. Partisan strife is the greatest single danger to our union. I wish it had never begun. I am told that it is in the very nature of politics and of humans themselves that they will divide into factions. There are even those who will tell you that in factions themselves and political parties themselves lie the very checks and balances that guarantee freedom. That is wrong, and they are leading you astray. We are all Americans; we all believe in the same Constitution, and you must avoid savage partisan political strife.

Union, the Constitution, a vigilant citizen body that avoids parties, and yes, a citizen body that is not only politically wise but is morally wise. The very foundation of freedom is liberty guarded by morality and religion. No nation will long endure if it is immoral. It must have a moral citizen body which rests upon the virtues of patriotism, frugality, honesty, and justice and which is educated for morality and religion. Those who tell you that you can separate freedom from morality and morality from religion are leading you down the road of despotism. You must always encourage institutions of education that will train future generations in the moral and political foundations of this country. Without religion, there will be no respect for oaths, no respect for any form of justice in this country.

As a final word, I urge us to avoid foreign entanglements. We must engage in commerce, and commerce means fiscal responsibility. In fact, part of morality is fiscal responsibility, that our credit always be good. Let us never borrow, but let us always have enough on hand to meet any emergency, including the possibility of war. Thus, we must have taxes. There are no taxes that are not inconvenient, but the taxes are the key to fiscal responsibility. Our commerce will flourish throughout the world. We should trade with every nation, and we should avoid political alliances with every nation. Hold every nation to be our friend, but make no foreign entanglements. Europe has an agenda totally different from that of our country. Providence has blessed us with geographical separation from Europe; it has blessed us with our own internal markets; it has blessed us with a continent across which we can expand. We have no need to become involved in political alliances with Europe. I would advise you never to have one nation as your friend always and in all times, and I advise you from antipathies on a constant basis with any nation, as well. Hold every nation to be your friend, have commerce with every nation, but do not make a single treaty or alliance based upon a permanent entanglement. Remember always the just war; defend yourself, but do not go abroad. These are my final words to you, my fellow Americans. I hope that we will all continue to prosper.

He went back to Mount Vernon and, there, was recognized even by former foes as the greatest man of his day. When he died, the ships of Britain and France were about to go into battle for the Napoleonic wars, and the French fleet suddenly lowered its banners. The British fleet signaled across and said, "What has happened?" The French signaled back, "General Washington is dead." Both navies lowered their flags and held an hour of silence in honor of this great man.

Lecture Thirty-Four
Abraham Lincoln, George Patton—War

Scope:

In the classical tradition of Greece and Rome, patriotism is defined by war. Our noblest deed is to die for our country. In his 1864 letter to Mrs. Lydia Bixby of Massachusetts, Lincoln gave a religious sanction to death in battle. The sons of Mrs. Bixby died so that the republic could live, and she herself had laid a "costly sacrifice upon the altar of freedom." For a later generation of Americans, the most significant embodiment of valor in battle was found in the life of General George S. Patton, another soldier who was willing to sacrifice his life and the lives of his men for his country.

Outline

I. Patriotism is a fundamental human value, and it has been fundamental to our own American experience. Abraham Lincoln (1809–1865) captured the deep meaning of patriotism in a letter written to a Mrs. Bixby of Boston, Massachusetts.

   A. Mrs. Bixby had lost five sons on the field of battle.

   B. Lincoln wrote to express his sorrow, as well as his admiration and respect, for a woman who had laid "so costly a sacrifice upon the altar of freedom."

   C. This profound statement came from a great president who hated war and had, in fact, voted against the Mexican War.

   D. Nonetheless, Lincoln led his country into the great struggle that was the Civil War and came to feel that the war was a punishment sent for the moral wrong of slavery.

   E. Lincoln's words carry us back to John 3:16. The everlasting life of the country, in the mind of Lincoln, was bought with the blood of such men as Mrs. Bixby's sons.

II. The generation of Americans who fought World War II had its most significant embodiment in the life of General George S. Patton (1885–1945). Patton exemplifies a true patriot and man of destiny who was also a mighty warrior.

A. Patton came from a long line of military men in Virginia. One of his ancestors was a Revolutionary War general, and his father and uncle had served in the Confederate Army.

B. From his earliest days, Patton wanted to be a soldier. He attended VMI, then West Point.

C. After graduating, Patton served in the U.S. Cavalry and was chosen by the army to compete in the Olympic pentathlon.

D. Patton went into the tank corps during the First World War and was wounded in action.

E. Patton formed a fast friendship with Dwight Eisenhower after the war.

III. When World War II broke out, Patton was chosen to be one of the commanders of the North Africa division.

A. Patton showed good diplomatic skills in dealing with the French government in Morocco and assumed command of the Seventh Army.

B. He was so successful as a commander that he was chosen to lead the next great Allied expedition into Sicily.

C. Though Patton made some controversial decisions, by August of 1943, he was the most celebrated fighting general in the U.S. Army. He was adept at the skills that make a great general—strategy, tactics, battlefield command, and logistics.

D. Patton's passionate dedication to his men and to the tenets of the army nearly cost him his position when word got out that he had threatened to shoot a man in a hospital for cowardice.

IV. Eisenhower stuck by Patton, partly out of friendship and partly because he was useful. Patton was sent to the north of England on a sort of nonsense task to organize and command a nonexistent army.

A. Patton's presence in northern England helped to convince the Germans that the invasion of Normandy would come at Calais.

B. Patton had served his purpose but was commanded to keep his mouth shut.

C. The invasion of Normandy was a success, but the American and British troops were tied down in the aftermath. Patton assumed command of the Third American Army and led one of the boldest attacks in history to drive the Germans from their positions.

D. By December 16, 1944, the Allied high command was convinced that the Germans were finished; only Patton doubted this assumption.

E. When the Battle of the Bulge began, Patton and his Third Army carried out one of the greatest winter marches in all of military history to rescue the 101st Airborne.

V. Though Patton was a tremendous success, he was considered dangerous. To keep him occupied, he was appointed military governor of Bavaria, a job for which he was not particularly well-suited.

A. Patton's comment that the Nazis were similar to the Republicans and Democrats made national news and essentially ended his career.

B. Patton was put in charge of the military unit writing the history of the war.

C. The great general was killed in a car accident in December 1945. His wife thought he should be buried in Arlington Cemetery, but he was too controversial. Instead, he was buried alongside his men in a military cemetery at Luxembourg.

Suggested Reading:

D'Este, *Patton: A Genius for War*.

Oates, *With Malice Toward None: The Life of Abraham Lincoln*.

Patton, *War As I Knew It*.

Questions to Consider:

1. Does it matter that Lincoln was misinformed about the number of sons Mrs. Bixby actually lost in the Civil War?

2. Was Patton a man of destiny?

Lecture Thirty-Four—Transcript
Abraham Lincoln, George Patton—War

We come now to Lecture Thirty-Four in our exploration of the life lessons we gain from the great books, and our theme in this final section is patriotism. Patriotism has certainly been a theme in some of the most important books ever written. Whether it is Pericles's Funeral Oration in Thucydides, the *Aeneid* of Virgil, or the historical plays of Shakespeare, patriotism is a fundamental human value—the love of country—and it has been fundamental to our own American experience.

At the time of the American Revolution, the American Civil War, and World War II, America brought forth an extraordinary group of leaders: the entire [generation of] Founding Fathers of our country, but above all, George Washington, Abraham Lincoln at the time of the American Civil War, and Franklin Roosevelt at the time of World War II. In each case—whether it's Washington, Lincoln, or Roosevelt—these statesmen were but the embodiment of the patriotism, the love of country, and the willingness to sacrifice of ordinary Americans. It was this patriotism that kept the army of Washington in the field; it was this patriotism on both sides that led brave men to grapple on the field of Gettysburg; and it was this patriotism that led American boys ashore at Guadalcanal or at Normandy.

This deeper meaning of patriotism was captured, above all, in a single letter written by Abraham Lincoln. It was written to a Mrs. Bixby of Boston, Massachusetts.

> Executive Mansion, Washington
>
> November 21, 1864
>
> Dear Madam,
>
> I have been shown in the files of the War Department a statement of the Adjutant General of Massachusetts that you are the mother of five sons who have died gloriously on the field of battle.
>
> I feel how weak and fruitless must be any words of mine which should attempt to beguile you from the grief of a loss so overwhelming. But I cannot refrain from tendering to you

the consolation that may be found in the thanks of the Republic they died to save.

I pray that our Heavenly Father may assuage the anguish of your bereavement, and leave you only the cherished memory of the loved and lost, and the somber pride that must be yours to have laid so costly a sacrifice upon the altar of freedom.

People who like to revise history and pull down great monuments, great individuals, and great writings—they have to attack this letter. You'll read sometimes it was written by a staff member of Lincoln; that's nonsense. Or they will point out—and this, to my mind, is the height of professorial arrogance—that Mrs. Bixby may not have had five sons who actually died in battle. It may be that only two of her sons—the professor will tell you—died on the field of battle. One died in a Confederate prison camp, one may have deserted, and one may have died in a prison camp or may have been honorably discharged. If she lost two sons, does that make the loss any less? Absolutely not. They will even cast aspersions on her moral character. What difference would that make?

This was a profound statement of a very great president who hated war; who when he was a congressman, voted against the Mexican War; who nonetheless led his country into this great struggle that was the Civil War. He suffered with every one of the 623,026 men—both Union and Confederate—who died in that war. He came to feel that the war was a punishment sent upon our country for the great moral wrong of slavery. He expressed this deeper meaning of war—"to lay a costly sacrifice"—because death in war becomes a religious act: to die so that your nation might live. Lincoln's words carry us right back to John 3:16, from one of our first lectures in the course: "God so loved the world that He gave His only begotten son, that whosoever believeth in Him shall not perish but shall have everlasting life." The everlasting life of this country, in the mind of Lincoln, was bought with the blood of these men.

The letter to Mrs. Bixby is a profound statement of the American ideal of patriotism. It was used as an important element in a movie—if we made movies into great books and called them great books, *Saving Private Ryan* would rank right up there—to explain, again, the loss, in this case of three sons, to one mother and the effort of the army to save the fourth from perishing.

That generation of Americans who fought World War II had its most significant embodiment in the minds of many of those men who fought their way across France in the life of General George S. Patton. Patton is one of the premier instances of a true patriot, who was also a mighty warrior and believed that he had a destiny. All our themes of the individual of destiny, finding that one unique mission that they have in life, the ideal of a patriot and of a man shaped by the great books—because Patton loved the great books—all come together in the life of George Patton.

He himself was the product of patriotism. His family had come originally from Virginia, and in fact, one of his ancestors was Hugh Mercer, a Revolutionary War general. Patton had both his father and his uncle, as well as several cousins, in the Confederate Army. In fact, one of these uncles—Tazewell Patton—was in Pickett's Charge, when those 17,000 men, on July 3, 1863, absolutely convinced that they were patriots serving the cause of freedom, made their way into the Union guns across three-quarters of a mile of a field. Tazewell was there with his cousins, and they were some of the very few Confederates to reach the final point in the Union lines, this little wall of stone. The Union soldiers on the other side so admired these Confederates that they said—reaching out their hands—"Come on over to the side of the Lord, brothers." The two cousins looked at each other, clasped hands, and leapt up on the wall, firing their revolvers. One was killed on the spot; the other, Tazewell, was lying there, and a Union officer took a final letter from him to the mother. Tazewell wrote, "My darling mother, I lie dying in a foreign land [Pennsylvania], but my final thought is of you and the deep love I bear for you."

Young Patton grew up on memories of this patriotism. In fact, he said that his mother kept beside him on the nightstand two pictures of bearded men. Until he was six years old, he thought they were Jesus and God, and then he discovered they were Robert E. Lee and Stonewall Jackson. From his earliest days, Patton wanted to be a soldier. His mother and his father read to him the tales of the *Iliad* and the *Odyssey*. He loved the *Nibelungenlied* and *The Song of Roland*, these gallant stories of knights of old.

He wanted to go to the United States Military Academy. His father was a man of some political influence out in California, where the family had migrated after the Civil War, but young George's scores—or "the boy" as his father always called him—were not very good, and he could not get into West Point. Finally, they decided that he could go to VMI, which is where his ancestors had always gone, where Tazewell had gone, [and] where Patton's own grandfather, who had been killed in action fighting for the Confederacy at the Battle of Cedar Creek, had gone. He was sent to VMI for one year; now isn't that facing adversity? Many people would have just given up and said, "It's not my mission to be a soldier." But no, he went to VMI, then got into West Point and promptly failed mathematics his first year. They were going to kick him out, but he pleaded and begged and stayed on another whole year. Finally, by 1909, he was ready to graduate. We even have his engineering textbook, and he wrote in the back of it, "last class, thank God." Then he goes on and lists what makes a good general, and at the very top is, "has to like to fight." That's the key: You have to like to fight.

He went into the cavalry and served out on the plains of the United States, riding in the path of men like George Custer, whom he admired tremendously. Then, in 1912, he got the opportunity to compete in the Olympics. In those pristine days, the Olympics were not the big show they are today [with] all the endorsements; they were still sort of a gentlemanly competition. He wanted to participate in the pentathlon, and he was chosen by the United States Army to participate for the Americans in the pentathlon. That is a traditionally military competition; it has saber fighting as part of it, dueling, pistol shooting, horseback riding, swimming, and also a marathon run.

The whole family, including Patton's father, who was absolutely devoted to "the boy," sailed to Stockholm. They arrived. Patton had cut out all alcohol, tobacco, eating only salads and steaks to get himself in shape. The first night he was there was the night before the pistol-shooting competition—which was his strength—and he wasn't used to the Sun being up all night. He didn't sleep, so he did very badly in that first competition. Again, you'd kind of give up, wouldn't you? Not Patton, no sir. He went into the dueling competition. Here, he was at a great disadvantage because these European officers were superb with the rapier. Patton went after them as though it was just another big sword and slashed and cut and slashed and cut, so he scored pretty high. Then he did better than expected in the swim, and then horseback riding was very good, and finally came the marathon. He set off [at a] dead heat, just running as hard as he could; collapsed right before the finish line; and the next thing you knew, his father was looking down over him and said, "Is the boy dead?" He wasn't dead and might have finished with a medal had there not been a dispute—which he never pursued—over his shooting. He claimed that two of his bullets had actually gone through the same hole, but he said, "In those days, we were gentleman. We took whatever decision was given to us." [They] didn't need to be tested, of course—he didn't add that, but we can add that—for any kind of substance abuse, and [he] went home without a medal but feeling he had done his best.

Then came the First World War. He was offered a staff position, which might have meant he could rise very fast, but he already understood that the new world would be based upon tanks, and he went into the tank corps. The Americans didn't even have any tanks in 1917, but he outfitted some Renault tanks that they got from the French; led his men into battle, firing his pistol from the very top of the tank; and was wounded in action. He saw also his first dead bodies. This warrior who sometimes is portrayed as so brutal wrote back [in] a letter: "They were lying there in the moonlight, British and Americans and French and Germans, all mixed up. I thought each one of them was someone's baby, some mother's son that she diapered, that she stopped from crying, that she held in her arms. What a terrible thing war is."

Then he returned to the peacetime army and formed a fast friendship with Dwight Eisenhower. He later said that the only contest he ever won with Eisenhower was whose hair would fall out first; he beat [Eisenhower] in that but in no other competition. Then came the next great war. Patton had seen it coming and had seen the important role that tanks would play in it. In fact, his very well-trained tank forces and his command had shown [it] in army maneuvers shortly before the war broke out. He was chosen to be one of the commanders of the North Africa expedition that landed in November 1942. Quite an extraordinary achievement: We were attacked by the Japanese in December 1941, very badly prepared, and by November 1942, we were launching an expedition into North Africa.

Patton was one of the commanders of that expedition which landed so successfully. He showed good diplomatic skills in dealing with the French government in Morocco. Then, on March 6, [he] assumed command of the Seventh Army, which had suffered a terrible defeat in the Kasserine Pass, one of the first big operations in which

Americans had come up against the Germans. He took over command of that army, and he whipped them into shape. He never minded using profanity; he never minded pulling cooks in and saying, "Why aren't you dressed in a helmet and a tie and leggings?"

"But we cook."

"You put on a helmet, a tie, and a legging, and you always carry your rifle with you. This is an army."

By the time he had finished with them, they were a fighting force, so he was chosen to lead the next great Allied expedition into Sicily. On July of 1943, with Patton in command, American troops, along with British troops under the command of General Montgomery, landed in Sicily. For Patton, war was serious business. He understood that; the Germans understood it. He had given his troops very clear orders: "War is about killing. You cannot trust the enemy when they surrender," so some of his men shot down surrendering Germans. There was some controversy about it, but Patton stood by his men and said, "This is what I told them to do."

He also got into trouble for leading his men ashore. General Eisenhower sent him a stern telegram saying, "George, your position is on the ship. You are not to storm ashore with your men."

"But that's the only way we can take the position," he said.

Politics played a big role in the war, and the British needed a great general; they needed to keep the home front well in support of this war, and General Montgomery was chosen to lead the most important push in Sicily. That was fine. Patton's job was just to hold down the flank. But he decided he would carry out a reconnaissance in strength, and so with his whole army, he went along the shores of Sicily, came up and captured the city of Palermo, and then, driving his troops hard, captured Messina before the British could get there. American troops now marched through the first major liberated area of Europe: Sicily.

By August of 1943, Patton was the most celebrated fighting general in the United States Army. He had those qualities that make a great general: [an understanding of] strategy, tactics, battlefield command, and logistics. Strategy: How do you win the war? Tactics: How do you win a battle? Logistics: Getting your men in place and your material in place to fight that battle. Finally, battlefield command:

What do you do when all your plans go awry? His strategy was clear to the capturing of Sicily, the very key to the Mediterranean area, and tactically, his landing at Gela—the first city in Europe liberated—was superb. He got his men in place; he always saw to it that they were well fed; and in battlefield command, he never minded going right up to the front, firing a colonel that wasn't doing his job, and replacing him with a second lieutenant who would get the job done. He also knew that these were rugged soldiers, and you talked to them in very rugged terms. His language—now I won't say all the words because I don't want you to get mad at me—but just one occasion, if I may use just one bad word.

The chaplain came up and said, "I just heard your speech, General, and it was just the worst language I have ever heard. Can you imagine the shock that our men feel about this? Don't you ever read the Bible?"

"Hell, yes. I read it every goddamn day, chaplain."

That's what he said, and that was his language.

In August, the most celebrated general in the army, he was visiting a hospital tent, and there, he pinned medals on the chests of brave boys who had been wounded in battle. He knelt beside and held in his arms some who would never see the next day. Then he came into a ward and there was a soldier there whimpering and crying. Patton, who was accompanied by the doctors and some nurses, went up to him and said, "What's wrong with you, soldier?"

"I just can't take it."

"What's wrong with him?"

"He has battle fatigue."

"Battle fatigue? What is that?"

"They called it shellshock in the First War."

"Yes, and it was a bunch of … then, and it's a bunch now! He's just a coward. He doesn't want to fight!"

"No, his nerves are shot."

So Patton slapped him.

Then, a few days later, he found another soldier doing the same, and he was more outraged because he was pinning medals on these brave soldiers and seeing the other soldiers who lay dead from their bravery. He slapped this one and said, "You're a coward; you ought to be shot. I'm going to shoot you myself," and he pulled out his pistol, but the doctors led him away.

This was serious, and the army tried to keep it quiet, but one of the nurses had a newspaper boyfriend, a journalist, and the newspapermen never liked Patton. They loved Eisenhower, they loved General Omar Bradley, but they didn't like Patton. He was a strutting martinet, more at home in the German army—they said—than in the American army. The story erupted, and Franklin Roosevelt himself wanted Patton brought home to lose his rank and his command.

Eisenhower—not out of friendship but simply because Patton was useful—stuck by him. But Patton, who would have been chosen to lead the great invasion at Normandy, was now sent on a nonsense task in England, where he was to organize and be in command of a nonexistent army stationed in the north of England. But it wasn't quite such nonsense: The Germans knew that Patton was the best general the Americans had, and the Germans were convinced that he was going to lead the expedition. The idea that somehow someone would not be chosen to lead an expedition because he had slapped a soldier was so patently absurd that the Germans put it down as just one more example of how inept the Americans were in coming up with spy schemes.

Patton was up there in the north of England. All this radio and telegraph traffic kept coming in and out about this army, and it made the Germans absolutely convinced that when the Normandy invasion came, it was going to come at Calais. Patton served his purpose, but he had one other order, and that was "Keep your mouth shut"; that is what General Eisenhower told him: "Keep your mouth shut."

He did, but he was supposed to be visible. One of his little tours was to go to a little town—Knutsford, it was called—where they were going to institute a new canteen for British and American troops. He was there, and the ladies of the town, serving their country in this way, asked Patton to give a little speech. He said, "No, I'm not supposed to speak."

They said, "Oh, please do."

He said, "Are there any newspaper people here?"

"No, there are no newspaper people."

He gave a speech, and in it, he said, "It is good that the Americans and British soldiers get to know each other better because after the war, we're going to rule the world."

"What about the Russians? What about the Russians?"

It's too late. There were newspaper people there, and again, it was blown all out of proportion.

This time, he got a demand from General Eisenhower: "You come to London." Patton arrived. Eisenhower brought him into his room—Eisenhower had a terrible temper—he's glaring at Patton. Finally, Patton got up—he had his helmet on—walked over, stood over Eisenhower (and Patton was a great, enormous man, well over six foot), and [Patton] said, "What was he going to do to me?" He stood up, and Patton put his head on Eisenhower's shoulder, and the helmet rolled across the floor. Eisenhower later wrote, "I always wondered what someone would have thought if they had come into the room at that moment." [Eisenhower said,] "George, you keep your mouth shut; do you hear me? I am not going to stand up for you again." But Eisenhower had to because he knew he needed a fighting general.

The expedition of Normandy was a success, but in the aftermath, the American and British troops were tied down in Normandy. Patton, on August 1, 1944, assumed command of the Third American Army. He led them on one of the most bold attacks in all of history, his tank corps sweeping ahead, driving the Germans from position after position, until by August 28, they had reached the Rhine River and Paris itself had been liberated. Germany seemed on the brink of absolute defeat. Then suddenly, there was no more gas for Patton's tanks. "Give me gas," he said, "and I can be in Berlin in a month." But it was a political decision. The Russians were to capture Berlin, and Patton waited.

By December 16, the Allied high command was convinced that the Germans were finished, that the Germans could not launch another major offensive. Only Patton doubted this, because he didn't listen to the information that came down through channels; he questioned German soldiers that were captured. He brought them into the questioning room and interrogated them: *"Wo waren Sie in Russland? Wo waren Sie in Russland?* ('Where were you in

Russia?') Look at that; look at that; look at the arms on him. That's a soldier. You hate me, don't you? He's a veteran from the eastern front; they are putting their best troops [out there], and they are going to attack one more time. Read history; the Germans always launch an attack when the darkness seems greatest. They'll launch an attack."

And so they did: The Ardennes Offensive, the Germans call it; we call it the Battle of the Bulge. The American high command was taken by absolute surprise as three German armies, the Fifth, Sixth, and Seventh, under superb generals, like "Sepp" Dietrich, Hasso von Manteuffel, and Erich Brandenberger, smashed into inexperienced American troops. They met in the great fortress city of Verdun, Eisenhower calling his generals together, a desperate situation.

He asked, "Can you or anyone hit the German flank?"

Patton said, "I will have my troops in action along all fronts in three days."

"It's a hundred miles over icy roads; don't be facetious, George."

"They will go into action," and so they did. The Third Army carried out one of the greatest winter marches in all of military history, coming to the rescue of the brave 101st Airborne and their bold commander, McAuliffe, who told the Germans "nuts" when they asked him to surrender.

Then, on across the Rhine, and just like Winston Churchill—you'll have to forgive me—Patton pissed in the Rhine. The Germans had brought this all on the world. And then, the war was over. Patton was again the most celebrated general in all of the American military at the time, the greatest fighting general, beloved of his troops. He was also a little dangerous because he had never learned to keep his mouth shut. He kept talking about, "What we ought to do is arm the Germans again and attack the Russians. They're our real enemy."

What do you do [with] somebody who's a total danger like that and you want to get rid of them, but you can't just fire them on the spot because they're too celebrated? You give them a job they are absolutely unsuited for, and so they made Patton military governor of Bavaria, which called for superb diplomatic skills, which Patton really did not have. He had gotten along well enough with the French, but this was beyond his capacity.

There he was [as] military governor, and he was faced with an enormously hard task. Germany was in absolute ruin:80–90 percent of its cities destroyed; a hard winter coming on, when you had to feed and keep people warm; and almost everybody, as he said, had been a Nazi. That's how you got any job, was to belong to the Nazi Party. He did what other military governors did: He let Nazis stay in their position if they could run a subway, or run the waterworks, or run the electric factory. But somehow the press picked on him, and they asked him again and again [for statements], and he was required to give press conferences. (That was another thing; he could not give a press conference. He could not sit there and let some newspaper person harass him as though he were a schoolboy.) There he was, one August day, and he didn't want to be there in the first place. His aides had made him hold this news conference, and he wanted to leave. He was going out the door when one of the newspapermen, who was particularly obnoxious and had been blowing smoke at Patton all during the meeting, popped up and said, "So would you say that the Nazis are sort of like the Republicans and Democrats?"

"Yeah, something like that," said Patton.

Oh, no. The newspapers got this. If it was a Republican newspaper, they said, "Patton Says Nazis Are Like Republicans." If it was a Democratic newspaper, they said, "Patton Says Nazis Are Like Democrats." This time, he was finished.

They put him in charge of the military unit writing the history of the war. There he was in Heidelberg on December 9, 1945, stripped of his command. His staff felt he was so downcast that they should maybe take him hunting. They were going out on a cold morning, this December 9; he was sitting in the back of his car, with one of those old-fashioned windows that let down between the driver and the back seat, with his favorite little dog, Willie—William the Conqueror—beside him. A truck pulled out in front of his car, the car slammed on its brakes, and he fell forward. The driver was absolutely unhurt, and he rushed back, and he could see that Patton's forehead was damaged, but it was worse than that: "I can't walk." They took him back to the military hospital. The finest neurosurgeon in the American army was flown over, but on December 21, uttering his last words, "This is a hell of a way to die," Patton passed away.

Patton's wife thought he would be taken back and buried in Arlington Cemetery, but he was too controversial, so she was told, while she was still over there in Germany, "He can't be buried in Arlington."

"Why?"

"The army's not taking people back to be buried there."

"That's nonsense; every day, they're taking back. … Of course," she said, "bury him with his men." He still rests in the military cemetery at Luxembourg, along with the brave men of the Third Army, who died to give us freedom.

Patton had one destiny in life. It wasn't to lead the great Normandy invasion; that required a general like Eisenhower, a master organizer. It was to lead his men in that one desperate struggle, starting in France, breaking the German lines, and then the Battle of the Bulge. [It was] to lead his men on that 100-mile trek to slam into the Germans, to come up against the finest infantry in all of Europe, and to see that the American soldiers that he had trained could take everything the Nazis threw at them and stop them dead in their tracks. "I am so proud of these men," he said. And so we should be proud of George Patton, a patriot and a man who found that one thing in life he was meant to do. May we all be so lucky.

Lecture Thirty-Five
Theodore Roosevelt—*An Autobiography*

Scope:

"Life is like a football game," Roosevelt said. "Hit the line hard. Hit it fair, but hit it hard." Theodore Roosevelt was a great patriot, a great president, and a great writer. His autobiography is probably the best such work written by an American president and teaches us a number of important life lessons. We learn to persevere. We discover that college is but the beginning of our learning experience and that our professors are frequently dinosaurs in their ideas. In moments of failure and despair, we must find strength in ourselves and discover our own version of a cowboy frontier. As citizens, we learn that an inexperienced politician and civil servant can become an effective president. Economics, he teaches us, is not a matter of doctrine but expediency. As a nation and as individuals, we should walk softly but carry a big stick. In his autobiography and his essays, Roosevelt defines patriotism and American values. Like Washington, Roosevelt tells us that our strength lies in unity, that liberty cannot be separated from morality, and that we must choose patriotism over partisanship.

Outline

I. In this lecture, we continue our exploration of the theme of patriotism in the great books. Is patriotism still for us today what it was at the time of the American Revolution, the American Civil War, or World War II?

II. Like George Patton and George Washington, Theodore Roosevelt (1858–1919) was another great American who believed in the nobility of dying for one's country. Roosevelt was one of the most successful presidents in our country's history, one of the greatest patriots, and one of the best authors. His autobiography is a testament to his talent.

A. Roosevelt was born into a wealthy New York family. His father devoted much of his time to charitable works.

B. Roosevelt took a broad view of our nation, had a deep respect for ordinary Americans, and above all, believed that the course of our country's history was unique.

C. Roosevelt graduated from Harvard and considered studying law but was troubled by the moral implications of an attorney's work. Instead he decided to go into politics and rose rapidly.

D. The death of his young wife was a terrible blow to Roosevelt. He left his daughter to be cared for by his sister because having the child near him was too painful.

E. Roosevelt then traveled west to the Dakota Territory, where he ran a cattle ranch. There, he came to the realization that it is ordinary Americans who make our country special, not the law firms or businesses of New York.

III. By 1889, Roosevelt was ready to return. He went back to New York, where he became police commissioner, was appointed by two presidents to serve on the Civil Service Commission, and was instrumental in instituting a civil service exam system in an effort to eliminate cronyism.

A. Roosevelt ran for governor and lost but was appointed assistant secretary of the navy.

B. The Spanish-American War was, in Roosevelt's eyes, a just war. He asked for and received permission to form a U.S. volunteer cavalry unit to assist in the effort.

C. On July 1, 1898, Roosevelt led the charge up San Juan Hill. Despite being outgunned, Roosevelt's cavalry unit captured the hill. Like Winston Churchill, Roosevelt believed that there was a glory to war that could never be made totally sordid.

IV. Roosevelt became a national hero and was swept into office as the governor of New York. He believed deeply in progressive politics; and in many ways, he was a Democrat in the Republican Party.

A. In 1900, some members of the Republican Party decided that the best way to keep Roosevelt quiet (and, perhaps, ruin him) was to make him vice president.

B. Roosevelt accepted the vice presidency under McKinley and quickly assumed the presidency after McKinley's assassination. He launched a bold political program that would enable him to accomplish more in office than almost any other American president.

C. Under the Square Deal, Roosevelt was one of the first presidents to examine healthcare, Social Security, and welfare benefits.

D. He also believed in a strong foreign policy. Roosevelt transformed the U.S. Navy into one of the strongest forces in the world. He believed that war was coming and that the United States would probably have to fight against enemies in Europe and Japan.

E. Though various companies had tried to build a Panama Canal for years, Roosevelt got it done.

F. In 1906, Roosevelt negotiated a peace treaty that ended the Russo-Japanese War.

G. He was awarded the Nobel Prize for Peace and, posthumously, the Congressional Medal of Honor.

V. At the height of his popularity, Roosevelt declared he would not run again for president. He had given his word and stepped down but saw to the nomination of his successor, Taft, whom he thought would continue his programs.

A. Taft proved a disappointment in this regard, and by 1912, Roosevelt was beside himself, having seen much of what he had gained squandered.

B. In addition to the loss of Square Deal programs, the country was unprepared for war.

C. Roosevelt campaigned for the presidency again but lost to Woodrow Wilson, a man Roosevelt considered a hypocrite.

D. As the Great War came, Roosevelt urged America to side with Britain and France. The articles he wrote at the time are virulent in their attacks on Wilson.

E. In 1918, Roosevelt received word that his son had been killed in action. He never fully recovered from the loss and died in 1919, at the age of 60.

VI. In Roosevelt's autobiography and essays, he leaves us a definition of patriotism that, like Washington's, still guides us today. He believed that Americans should put the country first and party politics second. He epitomized his philosophy of life when he said, "Life is like a football game. Hit the line hard. Hit it fair, but hit it hard."

Suggested Reading:

Roosevelt, *American Ideals.*

————, *An Autobiography.*

Questions to Consider:

1. How do you feel about Roosevelt's assertion that patriotism should come before partisanship?

2. Roosevelt emphasized the uniqueness of America as a country. What qualities do you think make Americans and America unique?

Lecture Thirty-Five—Transcript
Theodore Roosevelt—*An Autobiography*

We come to Lecture Thirty-Five in our study of the life lessons that we learn from great books, and we continue our focus on what we learn about patriotism; has patriotism been the subject of great books, which of course, it has; and is patriotism still for us today what it was at the time of the American Revolution, the American Civil War, or even World War II? George Washington stands before us always, as General "Light-Horse Harry" Lee said, "first in war, first in peace, first in the hearts of his countrymen." His Farewell Address is a call to patriotism. It speaks very little about war, because he knows that those who read his Farewell Address have been through that great trying period of war. But he focuses upon peace and upon the need for all of us to be Americans—not to be from the South or the North, not to be of the Republican Party or the Federalist Party, but to be all Americans.

George Patton is the prime example of a man who identified with his country, who loved it deeply, but who also found his greatest meaning in war. Like Washington, both Patton and those men who fought in the Revolutionary War, the Civil War, and I believe, in World War II—all of these would have agreed that the noblest thing you can do is to die for your country. Had you been able to go back to the battlefield of Gettysburg and ask the men on both sides, "What is the noblest thing you could do?" [they would say,] it is to die for your country. If you had asked their wives and sweethearts, "What is the noblest thing that can be done?" [they would say,] it is to die for your country. It is an interesting question if you ask it today to an audience—and it doesn't just have to be an audience of students; it can be people in their 60s and 70s—very few will actually raise their hands to agree that the noblest thing you can do is to die for your country. Yet Lincoln, in his letter to Mrs. Bixby, as in his Gettysburg Address, equated those who died for their country with the noblest of all sacrifices: that of Jesus.

Another very great American who believed that the noblest thing you can do is to die for your country is Theodore Roosevelt. The more I study Roosevelt, the more convinced I become that he is one of the most successful presidents in our country's history, one of the greatest patriots, and one of the best authors. In fact, of all our presidents, he is the most voluminous writer and his works still have enduring merit. John Kennedy, I think, was a very fine writer, and I think his *Profiles in Courage*, even his *Why England Slept*, are still very much worth reading. Richard Nixon's memoirs are interesting. Harry Truman wrote very spirited memoirs. But Theodore Roosevelt wrote some 20 volumes in his standard national edition, covering a range from American history, such as the War of 1812; through explorations of a river in Brazil; through comments on natural history, that is to say zoology; as well as an absolutely delightful and revealing autobiography. I don't know if you need to read modern big biographies of Theodore Roosevelt; go right to his autobiography and you will find the character of that man on every page. And on every page, you will find a tribute to patriotism and how important it is and his debt to the great examples from the past, such as Washington, Lincoln, and Robert E. Lee. In fact, he will frequently say that Robert E. Lee, George Washington, and Abraham Lincoln are the three greatest Americans.

Roosevelt was born into wealth, just like John Kennedy. He came from an old New York family, and some of the family members actually called it "Rooz-a-velt." You'll find many Americans from the turn of the century who always called him "Theodore Rooz-a-velt," but we'll just call him "Rose-a-velt" for simplicity's sake. His grandfather still spoke Dutch around the table and was a man of considerable wealth. Roosevelt would never have had to work in his life. He deeply admired his father. Roosevelt was born in 1858, and his father was a wealthy man who basically gave his life to charitable works and to organizing charities. Roosevelt said of his father in the autobiography, "My father was the finest man I ever met in my life." I like a person who says their parents are the finest people they ever met; that's real character to me, and I'm always dubious of people who lay all kinds of blame upon their parents. For Roosevelt, his father was the finest man he ever met, and his mother was the finest woman. She was a Confederate; "unreconstructed," Roosevelt wrote of her. Her name was Bullock; you can still visit Bullock Hall in Roswell, Georgia, where she grew up.

When he was a little boy of about four, he would say his prayers every night and ask that God protect his relatives who were serving in the Union Army and his relatives who were serving in the Confederate Army, who were admirals in the Confederate Navy. Roosevelt grew up to admire both the North and the South, and one of his most moving speeches was to the veterans of Vermont on the

40th anniversary of the beginning of the Civil War, in which he talks with such pride of the valor of the men in gray and blue and how our country had reconciled. From the very beginning, with this Confederate and Union background, Roosevelt took a broad view of our nation, had a deep respect for ordinary Americans, and above all, believed that the course of our country's history was unique. The Civil War itself was a statement of this uniqueness—this bitter war to rid our country of a moral wrong—and then at the end, instead of vicious persecution, guerilla warfare, the two sides reconciled. I think it is almost unique in the annals of history.

Roosevelt went to Harvard; he was a fair student; he liked mathematics and history. Because he was sickly as a child, with asthma and poor vision, he had had a series of tutors and had never quite gotten that firm foundation in Greek and Latin that the boys at Harvard, who had gone to private schools like Exeter and Andover, had gotten. He didn't like Greek and Latin that much, but he could still, as an older man, turn a Greek or Latin phrase. But he loved history and he loved mathematics.

He graduated from Harvard in 1880 and thought about studying the law, which is what his father wanted him to do. But he said: "After a brief period of law school, I began to worry about the moral implications of being an attorney. *Caveat emptor*: 'Let the buyer beware'; both in the business world and in the legal world, that seems to hide a lot of chicanery. The idea that a lawyer twists the law, the same way a businessman may twist the business world in order to get a profit, just struck me as something I did not want to do. Of course, the great amount of attorneys of our day [he said] were corporate lawyers, and they seemed to twist the law even more. "Instead, to the dismay of my father and some friends, I went into politics. Now you want a dirty business, they told me, it's politics. New York politics in 1880 were very dirty—machine, corruption— but I went into it because I believed you could make a difference, and if well-meaning patriots went into politics, maybe they would cease to be dirty."

He rose very rapidly; he was elected to the New York State legislature and became a rising young star. Fairly early on, he made a principled stand; that is to say, he was part of the progressive group within the Republicans, and they were for getting rid of all the old machine politicians. But the party nominated James Blaine, and he was a corrupt politician. But Roosevelt said, "We fought against nominating him, and now that he has been nominated, I will stand with the party." All the progressives turned [Roosevelt] down, and then his wife died. The death of his wife struck him so bitterly as a young man—they had a daughter, and she died shortly after the daughter was born, Alice—Roosevelt could never think about his wife again. He gave the little girl up to his sister mainly to take care of because even having her around was too painful for him.

He went out to the West, to the Dakota Territory, and "Without Dakota I never would have been president," he said. He ran a cattle ranch—still visited—out around Medora, North Dakota, out in the North Dakota badlands. His description in the autobiography—the little two-room cabin that he built, the cottonwoods blowing gently in the breeze, and living the life of a cowboy—it was there he began to understand what made America special. It wasn't the big law firms and businesses of New York; it wasn't Wall Street; it was ordinary Americans, the kind of frontiersmen he met in the day when he said the Wild West was still alive. Sheriffs who carried two guns and couldn't quite remember how many men they had shot dead. Going after a man who had stolen his boat, just pursuing him to show the man he couldn't steal his boat; capturing him; and then [being] so far away from a town, he had to stay up 40 hours straight guarding the man to make sure he didn't escape or kill Roosevelt. And the whole time, he read Tolstoy while he was watching this desperado. Or going into a barroom—he wore spectacles, and this immediately set the toughs upon him, the local hoodlums. This one came up to him and began to taunt him and said, "You are going to have to buy drinks for everybody." Roosevelt said, "OK, I'll buy drinks for everybody; let me get up and do it," and he shot the man a strong right hook, laid him out cold, and then went to bed.

That is the kind of life that he lived and won the respect of the cowboys. They were handy with the axes, particularly two of his own hunting guides he had brought from Maine. One of them said— he overheard them one day—"How many trees did you cut down today?"

"I got 60; how many did you get?"

"Forty-seven."

"How many did the boss get?"

"He beavered down 17."

Roosevelt said, "If you've ever seen what a beaver does to a tree, you can see how different my wood cutting was from them, but I learned."

By 1889, he was ready to come back into the world. In other words, like other figures we've studied, he had to go away, be on his own, find himself, and he realized that his destiny did lay in politics. It is most interesting that this most unconventional of presidents was a professional politician and civil servant. He became police commissioner of New York and cleaned up probably the most corrupt police force. He walked the beat with officers; learned which ones were really doing their jobs, which ones weren't; smelled their breath to see which ones had been drinking; [went] into local brothels to find out what police officers were hanging out there; and he cleaned it up. He served on the Civil Service Commission—[was] appointed by two different presidents to serve on the Civil Service Commission—and was instrumental in instituting an exam system. Roosevelt said an exam system does not solve everything, and there are offices in the civil service that probably shouldn't be filled by exams, but at least it was one way of getting rid of cronyism. He got his hands dirty, and he got a lot of criticism for it; there's no way to get into bigger trouble than [by] trying to reform a civil service organization or, indeed, trying to clean up a police force.

He ran for governor and lost, then was appointed assistant secretary of the navy. He was interested in the navy. His first book, long before all this began, had been a history of the naval War of 1812, a very fine study of it. He had studied deeply the teachings of Admiral Mahan at the United States Naval Academy, who taught the overall importance of naval power: No nation had been a superpower without a navy, whether it was the Athenian democracy, the Roman Republic, or whether it was Britain itself. France's failure under King Louis, as well as under Napoleon, was the result of their failure to be a naval power. Roosevelt studied all of this deeply, and he had the good fortune—he wrote—that the actual secretary of the navy was lazy and didn't do anything, and Roosevelt just took charge. He began to reform the navy, and he began to see that young officers coming out of Annapolis were promoted; thus, he began to build up the United States Navy. He began to be convinced that we had to go to war with Spain, and when the *Maine* was blown up in Havana

Harbor in 1898, Roosevelt looked upon it as a great deliverance for him.

The war against Spain—what we call the Spanish-American War—to my mind is a very good example of a just war. I frequently have people tell me, "Such and such a war is not just." Going back in our philosophical tradition, right back to St. Augustine or back to Cicero, a just war is: (1) a war that you undertake to protect yourself, or (2) it's a war you undertake to protect your allies, or (3) it is a war you undertake to overthrow a corrupt government. The colonial government of Spain was corrupt; it was very brutal, [committing] atrocities against the Cubans, who were trying to gain their freedom. And so we undertook, in Roosevelt's eyes at least, a just war. He wrote for permission and said, "Can I form a United States volunteer cavalry unit?" He had as the officer in charge Leonard Wood—they had struck up a very close friendship while he was there in Washington—and Wood was the commander and Roosevelt was second in command, with a title of lieutenant colonel.

This was going to be an unusual regiment. A request went out to territorial governors in places like Arizona, New Mexico, Oklahoma in Indian Territory, up into the Dakotas: We want men; we want men who can ride and can shoot, and we'll gather in San Antonio. And so they came: cowboys from the Plains, horsemen since they were little, crack shots, tough, and they were intermingled with football players from Harvard, Yale, and Princeton, the best of the day, Roosevelt said. They got along famously. First, they trained in San Antonio, where Roosevelt had served three years in the National Guard. He said, "This stood me in good stead. I knew how to drill them; I got them in good shape in terms of marching—they could already shoot anybody out of their saddle—and then we went off to Tampa by train and then off to Cuba."

There, on July 1, 1898, Colonel Roosevelt led the charge up San Juan Hill. They had been under heavy Spanish fire, and the Spaniards had a well-trained army; they had better artillery and better rifles than the Americans did. The Americans were still using old-fashioned Springfields; the Spaniards had the most up-to-date German Mausers. They were laying down a very heavy fire power on the Americans; the regular troops were entrenched and didn't want to move out. Roosevelt took his Rough Riders—his volunteers, First U.S. Volunteers—along with units of African American forces, the African American soldiers, and led them upward, and he asked the commander of the regular troops, "Can we go on and attack?"

The officer said, "I don't have any orders to do that."

Then Roosevelt said, "Will you let my men go through then?"

The officer said, "Well, I guess."

Then his own men—the regular troops—got so upset that they went, too. Roosevelt led them right up San Juan Hill—Kettle Hill, named from a big sugar kettle that was there—and in the face of very heavy Spanish fire, they captured it. Then Roosevelt led them to the next ridge. "San Juan," he said, "was the greatest single day of my life: all those brave men attacking together and the thrill of battle." Like Winston Churchill, Roosevelt believed that there was a glory to war that could never be made totally sordid.

Roosevelt became a national hero. He came back and was swept into office as governor of New York. He believed deeply in progressive politics. He was a real Democrat but in a Republican Party. He believed, [first], in the recall: If you don't like what a congressman is doing, you don't need term limits; you just recall him. He believed in the national referendum. In fact, he believed that if the Supreme Court declared unconstitutional a law, the American people should hold a referendum, and if they decided it was a law, it would be a law. He believed in the income tax. He believed in the direct election of senators. He believed that our country was in the hands of large business interests, who through their huge campaign contributions, corrupted every aspect of public life. He was not popular with a lot of Republicans.

As 1900 came around, the spinmaster of his day—Mark Hanna was his name, the great power behind the scene—and the other real movers in the Republican Party decided: What could they do to shut Roosevelt up? Of course, the best thing was to make him vice president; that would ruin him forever. He accepted under President McKinley to be the vice president, but in 1901, McKinley was assassinated. Roosevelt had been on a hiking expedition with his family when he got the news, and suddenly, Mark Hanna declared, "That damn cowboy is in the White House." Sure enough, he was. He began on a bold political program that would enable him to do more in office probably than any American president. At the start of it was, of course, to clean up politics.

From the beginning to the end, he had deep support among ordinary Americans; many of them voted Democratic, in most cases, in places like Oklahoma, but they supported Teddy. He hated the name Teddy. His friends called him Theodore, but that's what the Americans called him and that was good enough. It was Teddy. He believed in giving them a "square deal." He is one of the first American presidents to talk about healthcare, one of the first American presidents to talk seriously about Social Security, one of the first American presidents to talk seriously about welfare benefits, and he believed in a strong foreign policy.

Our navy was one of the weakest navies in the world, and when he left office, it was one of the strongest navies in the world. He thought we might never catch Britain, but we could certainly keep up with Japan and Germany. He sent the Great White Fleet, as he called it—16 mighty vessels—on a tour all the way around the world. In Japan, the Japanese saw the might of the United States Navy. But of course, there was one problem with having a navy and being the United States: He had ships on the Atlantic Coast, he had ships on the Pacific Coast, and it was a long voyage around South America to bring them together. He believed that war was coming and the United States would probably have to fight not only in Europe but against the Japanese. For years, various companies—particularly French companies—had tried to build a Panama Canal. Roosevelt got it done.

Some people might cast some aspersions on the way in which Panama became an independent country, but it became an independent country, and the Colombian regime—as he showed in his autobiography—was utterly corrupt. There had been 52 insurgencies and riots in Panama in 52 years, all protesting against the Colombian government's corruption and oppression. They wanted to be free; we let them be free. And then, he got that canal going. Despite yellow fever and terribly difficult terrain, that canal was built, and Roosevelt was there at its inception. Even going down—the first time an American president had actually left the United States during his term of office—to drive the big bulldozers because he loved publicity. He even loved the little teddy bear that people created in homage to him. A foreign policy, he said, must rest on walking softly and talking softly but carrying a big stick—maybe the opposite of some more recent American foreign policy decisions.

You had the strength—you didn't abuse it—but when you needed it, it was there and the world listened to you.

In 1906, the Japanese and Russians listened to him, and he brought them to Portsmouth and there worked out a peace treaty that ended the bloody Russo-Japanese War. He received the Nobel Prize. In fact, Roosevelt is the only American president to receive the Medal of Honor. He was nominated for it right after San Juan Hill, but he was too unconventional for the army and they blocked it. But later on, maybe 100 years later, he was granted posthumously the Medal of Honor. He won the Nobel Prize in Peace and he won the Medal of Honor. That's quite an achievement in itself.

Then, at the height of his popularity, he declared in 1908 that he would not run again. It was a decision that wounded him deeply. In 1904, he won the election on his own—in other words, he had become president from being vice president, [but] in 1904, [he won the election] by an enormous landslide. In fact, it was difficult to even find a Democrat to run against him; he won this huge majority. But he [had] turned to some newspapermen there in the White House and said, "Well, that does it; I'm not going to run again." He felt beholden to keep that promise. Now, can you imagine that today? Roosevelt said honesty is at the very heart of your life, and it was honesty that he admired in Washington and that he admired in Lincoln. His biography of Washington is short, but it is one of the most moving biographies. Washington, he said, was a man of complete honesty, of honor, not just in his public life, not just in keeping his word to others—that goes without saying—but he was honest with himself. He recognized his limits, he recognized what he could achieve, and to be honest with yourself sometimes is more difficult than to be honest with others.

He had given his word, and he stepped down. He really saw to the nomination of his successor, President Taft—300 pounds of solid Republican—and he thought that Taft would continue his program. But Taft, no, Taft was very much in the pockets of the big campaigners—the big campaign funders—and he was very much a man who believed that the country should stick to business. By 1912, Roosevelt was absolutely beside himself. He saw much of what he had gained being squandered; much of the Square Deal that he had brought to Americans [was] being passed away, and the country [was] still not prepared for war. He had gone off to hunt in Africa, and his journals of that trip themselves are marvelous studies of natural history, and courage, and just in wit, as well.

By 1912, he had had enough, and he wanted to gain the Republican nomination. The trouble was [that] the places where he was most popular, like Oklahoma, really didn't vote Republican in the primaries, [so] he lost. He had the great decision, and he bolted; he bolted the party [and formed] the Bull Moose Party, the newspapers called it; its real name was the Progressive Party. He stumped all around the country; it had been the tradition not to go out and campaign, but he went out and campaigned. On one occasion, he was actually shot by an anarchist and the bullet passed into him while he was getting ready to speak; it went into his speech, which was 50 pages long—he always had these long speeches, which he never gave—and then into his spectacle cases. It penetrated a little bit into him, and of course, his staff was there and was going to take him to the hospital. He got up and said, "Now, I don't know if I can finish," to the crowd, "but I'm going to speak because I've been shot, as some of you may have heard." He went on for an hour and a half. Now that's raw courage, and the American people admired it. But he lost, Woodrow Wilson became president, and the Great War came.

Roosevelt believed that Woodrow Wilson was the worst possible president. To him, Woodrow Wilson was a total hypocrite, and nothing is farther from a man of honor than the hypocrite. Cicero himself said that the hypocrite is the worst of all immoral creatures because he or she wraps himself in the cloak of honesty. All of Wilson's speeches about being neutral in mind as well as in action, to Roosevelt, were simply turning the back upon the important question. Germany was an immoral nation; its attack upon Belgium had shown that the Germans had no regard whatsoever for the most fundamental morality, [not to mention] the treatment of the Belgians. The United States needed to be on the side of Britain and France, and he spoke again and again, and his articles that he wrote at the time are virulent in their attacks upon the hypocrite Wilson.

Finally, at the sinking of the *Lusitania* [and] with the Zimmerman Telegram offering to give Mexico back the Southwest, America entered the war, and the final hypocrisy was Wilson's speech about leading this great and peaceful nation into war. Roosevelt immediately wrote and said, "I want to raise a unit of cavalry." They chuckled over this in the White House, and he fumed and fumed, but his sons enlisted.

In 1918, he got the word that his beloved son Quentin had died, killed in action, a pilot. He never fully recovered from that, dying in 1919, only 60 years of age. But in his autobiography and in essays like *American Ideals*, he leaves us a definition of patriotism that, like Washington's, still guides us today. "What is an American?" Roosevelt asked. "He is a patriot, and above all, he believes that it doesn't matter to what party a man or woman belongs. Are you a patriot? That is the question I ask. Do you put your country above parties? Do you put it above campaign contributions?"

He had very little use for the labor agitator, as he called it—the person who was always finding bad things wrong with America—but he had no use whatsoever for the businessman whose only fatherland, Roosevelt said, is the till, whose only fatherland is the cash register, or the bottom line, as we would say today. "Don't tell me you're a German-American or Italian-American or an Irish-American. I don't want any hyphenated Americans. We are all Americans. Come from wherever you want to," he said, "but once you are here, you celebrate the Fourth of July, not St. Patrick's Day."

Then, he believed deeply in the uniqueness of America. His book *The Winning of the West* is the highest tribute to the frontier and to the role of the frontier's men and women in spreading democracy across the continent. He admired the Native Americans—he had lived among them—but he believed that the spread of American democracy and freedom was providential. He was willing to see us take control of the Philippines because we would ultimately give them independence and ensure a tradition of freedom among them. Our country was unique, as Washington was unique, and as the ordinary American was unique. He epitomized his philosophy of life when he said, "Life is like a football game. Hit the line hard. Hit it fair, but hit it hard."

Lecture Thirty-Six
The Wisdom of Great Books

Scope:

Theodore Roosevelt, whom we studied in the last lecture, returns us to the theme of this course. He agrees with us that every educated person should read, but no one can prescribe a list of great books. We should decide individually what books speak to us, keeping in mind that our experience with books will change at each stage of our lives.

We have seen in this course that our lives should be based on certain fundamental principles, perhaps the most important of which is wisdom. Wisdom is different from information and knowledge. Information is facts and figures. Knowledge is using those facts and figures to gain a coherent picture of a subject. But wisdom is applying information and knowledge to the great decisions of life. Wisdom comes only with thought. It is the product of solitary communion with great minds.

Great books teach us to emulate those unconquerable spirits—like Seneca—who refuse to compromise their principles. Great books can lead us to apply wisdom to each stage of our lives, from youth to old age. In reading great books, we come to understand the power of love, for good and ill; we share the excitement of adventure and learn from those who have had the courage to change history; and we learn to see ourselves as others see us, to appreciate laughter and irony to put life into perspective. Great books also lead us to question the values and principles on which we make decisions as citizens. Great books are the most enduring school for life.

Outline

I. We come to the last of our lectures exploring the life lessons that we glean from great books, and we reflect on what we have learned. One of our guides in defining a great book is the Medal of Honor winner and president we looked at in the last lecture, Theodore Roosevelt.

A. The idea of a five-foot shelf of classics that every educated person should read was popular in Roosevelt's time. But Roosevelt believed that people should read whatever appeals to them.

B. The first step in loving great books is to pick the books that appeal to you. There is no such thing as a universal canon.

II. We have set up criteria for marking the great books worthy of our attention.

A. A great book should have a great theme, a theme that is noble in itself and will help inform decisions in life.

B. A great book should be written in noble language. It can be clear and forceful, lyrical, or intense, but it should be language that elevates the soul.

C. A great book should speak across the ages.

D. The historical circumstances in which authors write are also important. As readers, we should seek to know the history, know the author, and know the tradition.

III. Ultimately, we read the great books because they exemplify principles by which we should live our lives: wisdom, justice, courage, and moderation. These fundamental principles make up the essence of the tradition of the humanities.

A. In our world today, we are overwhelmed by information, but true wisdom is lacking. Ultimately, wisdom comes from using information and knowledge to make the important decisions in our lives.

B. We might define justice as how we deal with other people, and we have seen the foundational statement of justice running from the Gospel of John through Theodore Roosevelt and George Patton: Do unto others as you would have them do unto you.

C. Courage is found in knowing what is right and defending it, leaving the world a better place because you stood by your principles.

D. Our lives must also be tempered by moderation, and with wisdom and courage, we will know for ourselves whether our actions are immoderate.

IV. We study the great books in this Humanistic tradition because they make us better as individuals and as citizens.

    A. Perhaps many global mistakes could be avoided if our leaders read and pondered great books. Lawrence of Arabia, for example, believed that the West would never understand the Middle East because we refused to study Islam or Judaism and accept the intensity that religion has always had in that part of the world.

    B. Many of the themes that we saw in the political satire of the Athenian democracy can be seen in our society. We should learn from them before they become contemporary tragedies.

    C. One of the wisest lessons to be learned from the great books is to look at ourselves through the eyes of others.

V. The great books also teach us how to make life choices.

    A. Many of us might be tempted to follow the path of Thomas More, climbing up the career ladder but knowing, ultimately, that success is impossible. As we saw with More, that temptation can be fatal.

    B. And how will we deal with adversity when it comes to us? We can only hope to meet it with the courage that Thomas More did when he recognized his mistakes.

    C. It is also important to try to find our destinies. We should not become complacent or let adversity rob us of our ability to create or to act.

VI. Finally, the great books show us that our own country is unique. Perhaps the most important lesson of the great books is about freedom: freedom to make decisions, freedom to suffer, and freedom to gain wisdom. The great books are an inspiration and a guide to how to live our lives so that the world will be a better place.

Suggested Reading:

Adler, *How to Think About the Great Ideas*.

Denby, *Great Books*.

Fears, *Books That Have Made History: Books That Can Change Your Life*.

Roosevelt, *An Autobiography*, pp. 323–325.

Questions to Consider:

1. What is your definition of wisdom?

2. Is the unchecked flow of information over the Internet the friend or foe of wisdom?

Lecture Thirty-Six—Transcript
The Wisdom of Great Books

We come to the last of our lectures exploring the life lessons that we learn from the great books, and we reflect upon what, in fact, we have learned from the great books. We start with our definition of what a great book is. I think it is most interesting that our guide in defining a great book is a Medal of Honor winner and president of the United States, that is to say, Theodore Roosevelt. He read all the time, he could read one or two books a day and frequently did, and he read them in several different languages.

He was absolutely opposed, with his normal conviction, to a list of great books. "Nothing is more foolish," he said—and I entirely agree with it—"than a list of 100 great books or the five-foot shelf of classics." That was what was big in his day: the five-foot shelf of classics that every educated person should read. That's nonsense; you should read what appeals to you. One day, I might feel like reading Tennyson, and the next day, I might feel like reading Alexander Pope. "I don't like *Hamlet* particularly," Roosevelt said, "though there are portions of it I think are all right, but I love *Macbeth*. Why should I be forced to read *Hamlet* when I don't want to?" He said, "Let each individual pick what they think are the great books that speak to them, and know," as we have said in our class, "that each book will speak to you differently at each stage of your life."

Winston Churchill thought it was the greatest mistake in the world to have ordinary grade school and high school students read the *Odyssey* and the *Iliad*. "All that will do is make them hate it and they'll never go back to it. Let people come to these directly by reading books that they like."

Theodore Roosevelt said, "I don't particularly care for drama. It has to be about on the level of the Greek tragedies before I really like it, but that's my taste. I love good adventure stories. I love the *Nibelungenlied*," which we read in our class, "and I love *The Song of Roland*. They are good, vigorous stories," he said. You pick what books appeal to you. That is the first step in loving great books. There is no such thing as a canon that everybody should read. Don't let other people tell you what you should read because you are going to learn from it as an individual.

Nonetheless, we have set criteria that I believe do mark a great book and a book worthy of spending your time upon, and the first is that it must have a great theme. It must be a theme that is noble in itself, that will inform your decisions. We've studied the *Odyssey* and *Philoctetes* by Sophocles; we did read *Hamlet*, which I think is a great play; we read *Macbeth* and *Anthony and Cleopatra*; we read Roosevelt himself. His autobiography is the story of a great man who lived a great life and who made a great contribution. It is fully worthy to be considered a great book. A great theme: how to live your life; what moral values inform your decisions as you go through life; what is true courage; how do you succeed in overcoming, [for example,] all of the horrible, senseless pain caused by the Nazis if you are a young boy, [like] Elie Wiesel. Those are great themes.

And [a great book] should be written in noble language. It can be like the Gospel of John, written in clear, forceful, philosophical Greek prose. It can be like the magnificent lines of Seneca. It can be the wonderful poetry, lyrical in its intensity, of Aristophanes. But it should be language that elevates your soul. So much of what we read today, not to mention what we hear on television and in the movies, is filthy gutter language. There will be some obscenity in a play by Aristophanes, as George Patton understood the use of obscenity, but it's obscenity that makes a point forcefully. It is not a constant repetition of filthy words. A filthy repetition will simply make your mind filthy, whereas as is said in the *Tale of Two Cities* by Dickens, "There is nothing better than a good English 'damn' at just the right moment." Certainly, George Patton understood that, as did Roosevelt, as did George Washington. No soldier who served with him can forget crossing the Delaware in the swirling snowstorm on their way to Trenton and wandering around like a group of tourists asking, "What are we going to do next?" and his grabbing one by the shoulder—Washington—and saying, "Goddamn you to hell; stand by your officers." It was just the right language at just the right moment.

But we want noble language, and we want a theme that speaks across the ages. Every one of these books, I'm quite convinced, speaks to us now and will speak in centuries to come. Do you want one book from the 20th century that I believe will still move people 1,000 years from now? It's Elie Wiesel's *Night*. I believe that Schweitzer and his profound belief, [stated] in his autobiography, that we must have a reverence for life will be important as we go century into century in understanding how we really preserve our environment.

Books with a theme that speak across the ages and, then, to agree with Roosevelt, books that speak to you personally. At a particular moment in your life, it will be almost providential that you will reach on a bookshelf and pull up a work that says just what you need to know at that moment. That has happened to me when I pulled Isaac Singer's *The Penitent* off the shelf—never having heard of it before, having had no desire to read it—and sat engrossed as I read it through in one sitting.

Then, how do we approach these books? For these great books are the very essence of Humanism, and these are books that really have changed history. We have read Machiavelli, Thomas More, and Erasmus, all of them Humanists, all of them who were concerned deeply with human experience. Great books are the essence of the humanities for their goal is to teach us how to live our lives. We know we are going to die; we may believe the soul is immortal—we may not—but what matters is how we live that life before we die.

The Humanists of the age of the Renaissance—Erasmus, Thomas More, Machiavelli—they all believed in putting these books into a historical context, and that is what we have done in every occasion. What were the historical circumstances in which the author wrote that book? What were the works that he drew upon? What was his or her own life? How did the events of the life of Erasmus or Thomas More, wearing his hair shirt and scourging himself on a Friday, how did that affect his *Utopia*? Unless you know the history, unless you know who the author was, your attempt to read the book will be futile.

There was something years ago called the "New Criticism," which said just sit down with a text and read it. That's nonsense. You will miss one-half of what you can take away from that book. You must understand that it is part of a tradition: that Thomas More's *Utopia* is not fully comprehensible without Plato's *Republic*, that Seneca's masterful essays cannot be understood without knowing his mentor, the great Socrates. There is a tradition that builds, and the great books are part of that tradition. Know the history, know the author, know the tradition.

Ultimately, we read the great books because they give us principles by which we live our lives. The most fundamental of these principles is the essence of this tradition of the humanities: That is—starting with Socrates and going right on up to Theodore Roosevelt—that we live our lives based on certain fundamental principles, which are wisdom, justice, courage, and moderation. That is what Plato tells us in the *Republic*, that is what Socrates tells his students in his last meeting with them, his last class with them. We have spent all this time together learning that wisdom, justice, courage, and moderation are not names that people just give to ideas; they are realities. They are part of the very essence of God himself, and they exist as ideals with God, and we see only reflections of them here on this Earth.

Wisdom? Wisdom is something very lacking in our world today. We have a lot of information around us; that's what the Internet is filled with, all of this information. You are overwhelmed by it. It's what you see in the news, all these terrible things coming under [the picture], these little rolling scripts of horror each day: disasters, cyclones, catastrophes, murders. Then, we take some of that information and we might weave it into knowledge; that's what you'd do if you wrote a good essay based on this class. But ultimately, wisdom is using this information and knowledge to live your life and to make the great decisions that you have to make in life. Wisdom only comes about with solitude: Thomas More living for four years among the monks [or] Jesus going into the desert. That is where wisdom comes, and that is what our world most wants to deny us: solitude. We are so wired up, connected to everything, that we never have a moment to ponder. Don't read these great books unless you are going to walk and think about them. Take one in your hands—something you can't really do with that computer—and hold it and reflect upon it. Wisdom only comes with solitude and, as our tragedies taught us, perhaps with suffering. Only out of suffering can we learn wisdom.

Justice. Justice is how you deal with other people, and we have found one theme running all the way from the Gospel of John right on up until Theodore Roosevelt or George Patton: You do unto others as you would have them do unto you. It's fairness; it's the Square Deal that Theodore Roosevelt talked about, and it's what Thomas More talked about. He called government an organized conspiracy by the rich to plunder the poor. The very essence of Christianity, More and Erasmus said, as did Theodore Roosevelt and

Lincoln, is "Do unto others as you would have them do unto you." Lincoln asked Senator Douglas at the height of their debates, "Senator, are you a Christian?"

"Yes."

"What's the Golden Rule?"

"Why, do unto others as you would have them do unto you."

"Would you be a slave?" That is the answer that echoes all the way down.

Then, courage: Do you know what courage is? Courage is being fair to yourself; it's knowing what is right and standing up for it and leaving the world a better place because you stayed to your principles. Moderation: Much of our reading has been about moderation, making the right decision, prudence. Socrates knew it was the right moment for him to die. Albert Schweitzer knew it was not immoderate for him to go back to medical school and to go out to Africa; that was what his destiny was. Meriwether Lewis knew that when Jefferson offered him this great opportunity, there might be many who would say, "How foolish to go off into the unknown when you are right now private secretary to the president of the United States. Who knows what great things will be offered to you if you stay in this staff position?" But he chose that great destiny. When you are right and you are exercising that wisdom, you know it's not immoderate. Wisdom, justice, courage, and moderation—follow them as you go through life.

We study the great books in this Humanistic tradition; in the tradition of our Founders, as well; in the tradition of Joseph Addison's *Cato*, because they make us better as individuals, and they make us better as citizens, particularly as citizens of a free republic. We learn lessons right now today from these great books. Josephus and the story of the war of the Jewish people against Rome takes us right to the very heart of the Middle East. I frequently ponder how many mistakes could be avoided if our leaders and our nation as a whole simply bothered to read and ponder the lessons of the Middle East: the rich tradition of the Koran, the rich tradition of Judaism, and the deep intensity that religion has always held for that part of the world.

The Jewish people in the time of Rome had the easiest choice in the world, we would say today. Rome brought them Roman values, individual freedom, and the life of the city, what we would call Western values. It did it with a tolerant government that recognized their freedom to worship as Jewish people, and they cast it all away to undertake a war against the superpower of the day because of God and their firm belief that they must be a theocracy ruled only by God. The Romans called them terrorists, but to [Jews], they were freedom fighters. Lawrence of Arabia, that man of destiny, how immoderate it was for a lieutenant to go off into the desert of Arabia and think that he could raise up a revolt of Arabs that would change the war. He left behind as his legacy much of the political situation of the Middle East today: Iraq, Jordan. He, to the end of his days, believed that we in Europe and America would never understand the mind of the Middle East because we refused to understand Islam itself.

Politicians: I'm not sure that politics in the democracy has changed all that much since Aristophanes and the Athenian democracy. That kind of biting political satire is only possible among a truly free people. Just change some of the names from Cleon and Hyperbolus to names that might be in our news today, and you have the same scheming politicians, the same ordinary citizen willing to be hoodwinked, the same great military adventures that end up in disaster, and the politicians clamoring to have an office they don't know what to do with if they got it. Thomas More said it from the point of view of a monarchy: You have all these kings of France who want to also be king of Venice. They can't even rule France well—they've got all these internal problems in France, this economic transformation—but they want to go off and rule a people that doesn't want them at all. It does make you better as a citizen, at least, to say, "These are mistakes. We know they are mistakes; let's step back before they become tragedies."

But as an individual, can you learn from these great books? One of the wisest lessons I learned from the great books is to see myself with the eyes of others. That's why Greek tragedies, like the *Philoctetes*, are always set in the distant, mythological past: the age of the Trojan War. You see that these issues are enduring; they have been in all times and in all places. The role of the chorus is to tell an Oedipus, it's to tell an Agamemnon, it's to tell an Ajax: "This is a big mistake that you are making. You can't see it because you're so blinded. You suffer from *atē*, from moral blindness, and you are swollen in your *hubris* and your outrageous arrogance. You cannot see what a mistake this is, but [we] can."

In Praise of Folly has become one of my favorite books, as Erasmus is one of my favorite individuals. He was a man of great moral principle; he believed deeply in wisdom and he acquired wisdom. He believed that the life of Christ was a pattern, and if you had the life of Christ, you didn't need all the dogma of Christianity. Justice: He tried to deal with everyone on a just and even level, although he had a furious temper that sometimes came out when his books were attacked. He had courage, but he also had moderation. He refused to join the side of the Reformation. He believed in the Holy Church, he believed in the authority of the pope, and in his very moderation, he set a model for us of religious tolerance.

But his *Praise of Folly* is just that: stepping back and looking at the world and all the follies that we engage in. We could give them different names today. He talks about the folly of lawyers and how treacherous they are, but I happen to believe that the law and medicine are the two noblest professions you can follow. But what would Erasmus do if he came back today and said, "Why are you running around with that BlackBerry? Do you really need to be that connected?" Is that not the ultimate folly, to think that one more e-mail is going to change anything in the world or, in fact, that computer, on which you can write book after book after book and send them off to hundreds of people?

When Thomas More wrote his *Utopia*, he had one copy—he had written it by hand—and it had to go by a trusted messenger to Erasmus to see to its publication. Not today: You can send out all of these copies and every friend, every time you get an e-mail, you can send it to them, as well. Are we really any wiser? Absolutely not. We have a lot more information, perhaps, but we are not any wiser, and in fact, our political decisions suggest we haven't learned a single thing. So [much for] all our connectedness. I like to think that exercising is one of our follies. I continue to wait every day for medical science to reveal that the worst thing a person of my age can do is exercise. Just the way Thomas More scourged his body—and Erasmus said that was a bad idea—but Thomas More beating his back with whips—is that any different from dreading to go into some gymnasium, working out with these weights and all of this agony, walking around and around some track like some gigantic hamster? That's the folly that we torture ourselves in this life perhaps to gain another year or two of life.

Or the very folly, Erasmus would say when he attacked the university, of our whole idea that education is nothing but credentials. I always point out to my students, the only exam a professor never has an opportunity to talk about with students is the final exam, which ought to be the most important to go over with them. Instead, you've got that credential, [and] you're out. And so our universities [also] rest upon credentials and fundraising. What would Erasmus do with the development officers of today, where every aspect of our life—whether it's running for president or whether it's making a great university or even running a church—is measured on how much money you bring in. Our follies, Erasmus should be here to point them out to us. So see yourself as others see you.

Then, we learn from the great books how to make our life choices. It is most interesting to me how easy it is for us, at various stages in our life, to follow the path of Thomas More. Here was a man deeply learned in the great books, and step by step, he took a path that he should have known—and his friend Erasmus told him—was disastrous. But it was the next step up the ladder, and he had started out on that career of political favor. [He went] from being an undersheriff to being speaker of Parliament, to being in charge of the duchy of Lancaster, right on up to being lord high chancellor of England, knowing from the fall of Thomas Wolsey that the task that the king had set him was impossible: to get the pope to give an annulment to the marriage with Catherine of Aragon. The pope at the very moment was the prisoner of Emperor Charles, who was the nephew of Queen Catherine. He was not going to give an annulment, but More took [the position].

How many times will you or others that you know be called in by the CEO, made a vice president, given some task that you know is impossible, but you go ahead and do it and you fail disastrously? How then do you deal with adversity when it comes to you? I hope you'll deal with it the way Thomas More did because here was a man that had made a very big mistake, and then at the last, he decided he would stand up with courage. He went to that Tower of London, and his wife told him again and again, "You are crazy to rob us of a husband and a father when almost every other churchman in England has signed this concession that the king is the head of the church. What difference will it make?" But to More, this was his destiny, and he had finally discovered it. And so he died. Ultimately, [your goal is] to find your destiny.

We began our lectures with Seneca. Here was a man just like Thomas More, who had been beguiled by power, who thought he could change an evil ruler like Nero, and found himself caught up in even abetting the tyrannical schemes of Nero. But in the end, he had come to realize that his destiny was to die absolutely true to his principles. How many various officeholders existed under Roman rulers? We remember Seneca because he died for his principles. How many lord high chancellors of England can you name? But we remember Thomas More because he found his destiny. Ultimately, that's what great books can do if you open your heart to them: [help you] to find the one thing in life you were meant to do.

Most interestingly, no matter how old you are—you may not have achieved that destiny—[but] don't let anyone ever tell you you've done what you need to do in this world. [Don't just] sit back and build a house in Florida or in the Rocky Mountains. Cicero had every opportunity just to enjoy his last years. He even had important tasks, like getting his son back on track. He had written the most enduring, charming essay on all the merits of a quiet old age: not worried anymore by romantic attachments, not worried anymore about having an extra glass of wine at lunch, not worried about keeping yourself in shape, and absolutely not worried about the political situation. Had he not fulfilled everything that destiny might offer him: to have become the greatest thinker in the Latin language, to transform the Latin language into a vehicle suitable for transmitting the next thousand years of European civilization, and to make Plato and Aristotle understood by his fellow countrymen? Yet, at the old age of 63, he stepped forward and took up the challenge and would lay his life down for the freedom of his country.

Finding your destiny, whether it is that of a Meriwether Lewis, to open up whole new worlds, or of an Elie Wiesel, a young boy, 14 years of age, who sees his whole world collapse around him. His mother and sister taken off out of the same line that he stood in at Auschwitz, never to see them again. To see his own father die before his eyes, unable to help him. To give up his belief in God and the whole tradition in which he has been raised. Then, to come to believe that there was a reason for all of this suffering. That, too, the great books teach us. We may never understand why this adversity comes upon us. We may, like an Oedipus, try to justify what we did: "I didn't know I was marrying my mother. I didn't know I killed my father. I can't possibly have sinned." But Elie Wiesel said, "This has happened to me. I will not let it destroy me." Out of that misery, he would not only create a soul-stirring novel, but he would spend his life trying to bring peace to the Middle East, to reconcile Jew and Arab, and to dedicate his life to this purpose.

In the same way, a Roosevelt, a Lincoln, a George Patton, or a George Washington not only found their destinies, but they also show us, as I believe the final lesson of the great books is, that our own country is unique, that the Americans have been called to a destiny. We may fight against it; we may slip back time and time again, but as Theodore Roosevelt said, "There has never been a nation of people so kind, so magnanimous, so willing to forgive, and so willing to take up the challenge of bringing freedom to the world." Perhaps ultimately that's what the lesson of the great books is about, freedom: your individual freedom to make decisions, your individual freedom to suffer, and your individual freedom, ultimately, to gain wisdom. Life, liberty, and the pursuit of happiness, for the pursuit of happiness is all about your living your life in such a way that when you die, the world is a better place for what you did for those you touched. The great books are an inspiration and a guide to how you live your life so that the world will be a better place.

Timeline

B.C.

3000 ....Emergence of the first literate, complex civilizations, including literature. This takes place in Egypt and the modern land of Iraq (Mesopotamia).

2500 ....Great Pyramids of Egypt.

1250–1240.............................Trojan War.

1230 ....Possible date for the Exodus of the Jewish people out of Egypt.

c. 725.....................................*Odyssey* composed.

490–404.................................Golden age of Athenian democracy.

336–323.................................Reign of Alexander the Great.

218–146.................................Rise of the Roman Empire.

48–31.....................................Julius Caesar and Augustus establish monarchy at Rome.

A.D.

31 B.C.–A.D. 180 ....Golden age of the Roman Empire.

c. 6–36...................................Life of Jesus.

312–1453...............................Middle Ages.

476 ....Fall of the Roman Empire.

570–632.................................Life of Muhammad.

c. 742–814.............................Life of Charlemagne.

c. 1096–1099.........................First Crusade.

c. 1304–1527.........................Renaissance.

1509–1547.............................Reign of King Henry VIII.

1517–1648.............................Reformation.

1558–1603.............................Reign of Queen Elizabeth of England.

1648–1789...................................Age of Enlightenment.

1775–1824...................................American Founding.

1789–1815...................................French Revolution and the reign of Napoleon (from 1804).

1861–1865...................................American Civil War.

1914–1918...................................World War I.

1917–1991...................................Russian Revolution and the rise and fall of the Soviet Union.

1933–1945...................................Hitler rules Germany.

1939–1945...................................World War II.

1945 ....Scientific and technological revolution.

1948 ....Birth of Israel.

Glossary

Argonauts: In Greek mythology, the Argonauts were the heroes who sailed with Jason on the ship *Argo* to capture the Golden Fleece.

chivalry: The medieval complex of ideals that was to govern the conduct of a knight, including honor, courage, loyalty, and compassion for the weak.

classical antiquity: The historical period from roughly the rise of Greek civilization in the 2nd millennium B.C. to the conversion of Constantine to Christianity in 312 A.D.

classics: Conventional term to describe the study of classical antiquity. It is now used to describe all great books from all civilizations and time periods.

communism: The idea that society should be constituted so that the means of production and subsistence should be held in common and labor organized for the common benefit. Communism was taught by Plato and by Thomas More in his *Utopia*, but Karl Marx is the intellectual father of modern communism in modern times. The political system of modern communism has been marked by the creation of a totalitarian state and party apparatus to subordinate all aspects of life to the state.

courtly love: The late medieval ideal of love between a married woman and her gallant paramour. Strict conditions were imposed on how the affair could be conducted. But courtly love was not platonic. The themes and ideals of courtly love inspired poetry and prose romance novels.

Crusades: Military expeditions by Western Europeans of various nationalities to liberate the Holy Land from Muslim rule. There are generally said to have been eight Crusades, launched from 1096–1272.

Enlightenment: Conventional historical term to describe the period in European history from 1648 (the end of the Wars of Religion) to 1789 (the beginning of the French Revolution). The thought of the Enlightenment was marked by a belief in progress, science, and reason. The American Founding can be viewed as an event of the Enlightenment.

epic poetry: Long narrative poetry, dealing with great events, such as the *Odyssey*, *The Song of Roland*, and the *Nibelungenlied*.

feudalism: Political, social, and economic system of medieval Europe, resting upon the possession of land by a warrior nobility in exchange for their military service to a ruler or lord.

Founding Fathers, the: Conventional terms to describe the political leaders who shaped the American Revolution and Constitution. The Founding can be considered to have lasted from 1775 (the Battle of Lexington) to 1826 (the deaths of John Adams and Thomas Jefferson).

Humanism: The intellectual currents of Renaissance and Reformation Europe, based on the intense study of the classics as the models for literature, art, architecture, philosophy, and even politics. The classics focus on human knowledge as opposed to theology, hence the term "Humanism." However, the desire to use Greek and Latin to better understand and to reform Christianity was fundamental to many Humanists, including Erasmus and Thomas More.

Middle Ages: The period in European history from the conversion of the Emperor Constantine to Christianity in 312 A.D. to the fall of his city of Constantinople to the Turks in 1453.

Nazis: Followers of Adolf Hitler and his doctrine of National Socialism, which was the foundation of the German Third Reich (1933–1945). National Socialism was based on pseudo-scientific racism, socialism, and nationalism. It advocated the complete subordination of the individual to the goals of the state, which was identical with the German race. Fundamental to Hitler's goals was the destruction of the Jewish people.

Ottoman Empire: The dominant political structure of the Middle East from 1453 (the conquest of Constantinople) to 1918. The founder of the empire was Othman, hence the name "Ottomans." The Ottomans were Turkic people, originally from Central Asia. At the height of its power, the Ottoman Empire reached from Iraq to Vienna to Morocco.

Peloponnesian War: War between Athens and Sparta from 431–404 B.C., ending in total victory for Sparta.

Pharisees: Members of an influential Jewish group in the time of Jesus. Pharisees were professors of the Jewish law, who wielded enormous religious, cultural, and even political influence.

rabbi: A Jewish scholar and teacher, who may be the spiritual leader of a congregation.

Reformation: The attempt to reform the Catholic Church, leading to the rise of the religious beliefs of the Protestant faiths, including the denial of the supremacy of the pope. Conventional dates are from Martin Luther in 1517 to the end of the religious wars between Protestants and Catholics by the Treaty of Westphalia in 1648.

Renaissance: The conventional term for the historical period from the end of the Middle Ages to the Reformation. It was marked by a renaissance—a "rebirth"—of knowledge of classical antiquity and the application of the models of classical culture to literature, philosophy, art and architecture, and even politics. Convenient dates are from the influential Italian poet Petrarch (1304–1374), who revived the love of classics, to the beginning of the Reformation under Martin Luther.

Roman Empire: The political system that ruled the Mediterranean world and Western Europe from 48 B.C.–476 A.D. This is the empire of the Caesars, from Julius Caesar to the last Roman emperor in Italy, Romulus Augustulus, deposed by Germans in 476 A.D. Already in the 3rd century B.C., the Romans, under their republican government, began to acquire an overseas empire. Historians, rather confusingly, speak of the Roman Empire of the Republic. Julius Caesar and Augustus ended the republican form of government and established the military monarchy that governed the empire until its end.

Stoicism: Philosophical and religious beliefs developed in the 4th century B.C. by Zeno at Athens. The name derives from the Greek word *stoa*, which simply signified the covered porch where the philosophers first taught. Stoicism posited a single, all-powerful, all-beneficent God, who created the universe and determined all events. Happiness for the individual lies in accepting the will of God. Stoicism became one of the most powerful intellectual currents of the Roman Empire, culminating with the Roman emperor and Stoic thinker Marcus Aurelius.

synoptic Gospels: Scholarly term for the Gospels of Matthew, Mark, and Luke. It is derived from Greek "to see things in the same way." The term refers to the fact that these three Gospels have a common narrative, differing from that of the Gospel of John.

Talmud: The Rabbinical commentaries on the Jewish Law of the Old Testament. Compiled over a number of centuries, from the 2nd to the 6th centuries of the Common Era, the Talmud is second only to the Bible as the sacred text of Judaism.

tragedy: The conventional literary term to describe a play that ends sadly.

Trojan War: The 10-year war between the Greeks, led by Agamemnon, and the great city of Troy, which ended in the destruction of Troy. The theme of Homer's *Iliad*, the Trojan War was a real conflict fought around 1250–1240 B.C.

Yiddish: The common language of the Jews living in central and eastern Europe from the later Middle Ages onward. Yiddish is derived from a German dialect. It is written in Hebrew characters. It remains a living language with an extraordinarily creative literature.

Biographical Notes

Attila the Hun (c. 406–453): Conqueror. From war chief of the nomadic Turkic people called the Huns, Attila rose to become the most powerful and feared figure of the waning days of the Roman Empire in the west. A superb administrator, Attila created a multicultural, diverse empire in central Europe that held Rome as a tributary state. The savagery of his military campaigns led Christians to call him the "Wrath of God." Attila planned to conquer the whole of Europe, but he was defeated by Roman and Germanic troops at the Battle of Chalons in 451 and failed in his attempt to conquer Italy. He died suddenly on the night of his wedding to a German princess, leaving behind a reputation that influenced the *Nibelungenlied* and still resonates today.

Caesar, Gaius Julius (100–44 B.C.): Roman politician, military leader, author, and statesman. One of the greatest figures in history, Caesar rose from being an ordinary politician to become the savior of his country. His conquest of Gaul (modern France) from 58–52 B.C. changed the course of Roman and European history. His victory over the armies of Cato in 46 B.C. marked the consolidation of his dictatorship, gained by civil war. He transformed Rome from a republic into a monarchy and instituted reforms that ensured two centuries of peace and prosperity. His assassination in 44 B.C. plunged the Roman world into further civil war, from which his adopted son Octavian (Julius Caesar Octavianus) emerged as ruler. Known to Shakespeare as Caesar and to history as Augustus, Octavian's victory over Antony and Cleopatra in 31 B.C. secured his power and enabled him to continue the work of his father.

Charlemagne (c. 742–814): European statesman. From king of the Germanic tribe of the Franks, Charlemagne rose to become the most powerful political figure of the early Middle Ages. His coronation as Roman Emperor by the pope in 800 marked him as the heir of Julius Caesar and the legacy of the Roman Empire. His military expeditions created a vast empire in Europe. He revitalized culture and spread Christianity. The modern European Union rightly looks upon Charlemagne as one of the founders of its ideals.

Henry VIII (1491–1547): King of England. One of the most influential kings in English history, Henry was a scholar, well-educated in Greek and Latin, and an admirer of the Humanists, including Erasmus and Thomas More. His foreign policy made England a great power. In religion, he broke with Rome over his desire to have an heir to the throne and, hence, to divorce Queen Catherine, who had not produced such a child. Henry promoted and enriched Thomas More, who was his willing servant until the king and Humanist clashed over matters of conscience.

Hitler, Adolf (1889–1945): German dictator. Hitler rose from obscurity to be absolute ruler of one of the best-educated and most industrious nations in the world. As Führer ("leader") of Germany, he established a totalitarian state based on the doctrines of National Socialism. In his book *Mein Kampf* (*My Struggle*), Hitler clearly laid out his plan to begin another world war and to destroy the Jewish people. The world refused to listen, and Hitler began the war in 1939. His determination to destroy the Jews fundamentally shaped his military strategy. He died a cowardly death by suicide in his bunker in Berlin on April 30, 1945, with the blood of 50 million people on his hands.

Luther, Martin (1483–1546): German religious leader and theologian. As a Roman Catholic monk and professor at the University of Wittenberg in Germany, Luther applied the knowledge of the Humanist Erasmus to the study of the New Testament. He became convinced that Catholic doctrine was wrong in fundamental questions that affected the salvation of the soul. He challenged the church and was excommunicated. He became the leader of a movement called the Reformation that changed forever the politics and culture of the world.

Stalin, Joseph (1879–1953): Russian dictator. Stalin ranks with Genghis Khan as one of the most successful and bloody-handed tyrants in history. An ethnic Georgian, Stalin became a convinced Marxist early in life. He rose to play a prominent part in the Russian Revolution. After the death of Lenin in 1924, Stalin outmaneuvered all his rivals, including Trotsky, to become absolute master of the Soviet Union. His policy of systematic terror killed perhaps 20 million of his fellow citizens. He led the Soviet Union to victory over Germany in the Great Patriotic War (World War II). He died in bed, leaving his country master of an empire and a nuclear superpower.

Theodoric (454–526): Germanic war chief and king. Theodoric began his career as war chief of the Germanic tribe of the Ostrogoths, then rose to be called king of Italy and recognized as such by the Roman emperor in Constantinople. He was one of the most powerful and influential figures of the early Middle Ages. From the Italian city of Ravenna, he ruled a multicultural and diverse kingdom of Germans and Romans in Italy. He was a Christian and patron of culture, leaving behind notable works of architecture. He was a law-giver and administrator, who brought a degree of peace and prosperity to Italy. But he was also a bloody tyrant, willing to use terror and murder whenever it suited his purpose.

Tiberius (c. 42 B.C.–c. 31 A.D.): Roman emperor. The adopted son of Augustus, Tiberius succeeded as emperor and absolute ruler of the Roman Empire. A capable soldier and administrator, he was the Roman emperor who most resembles Stalin. He used systematic terror to maintain his complete control of all instruments of power. He was suspicious to the point of paranoia. Like Stalin, he used the charge of treason to destroy any figure he thought might be a threat. He was emperor when Jesus was tried in Jerusalem. The personality and policies of Tiberius played a fundamental role in the decision of the Roman governor Pontius Pilate to execute Jesus.

Trotsky, Leon (1879–1940): Russian revolutionary. Trotsky played a fundamental role in bringing about the Bolshevik triumph. He was an intellectual and powerful orator, who proved himself a military leader of remarkable ability in organizing the Red Army and its victory in civil war. As ruthless as Lenin and Stalin, Trotsky lost out to Stalin. Sent into exile, he wrote savage attacks against Stalin and was killed on Stalin's orders in Mexico.

Bibliography

Ackroyd, Peter. *The Life of Thomas More*. New York: Doubleday, 1998. A good biography for the general reader.

Addison, Joseph. *Cato: A Tragedy, and Selected Essays*. Indianapolis: Liberty Fund, 2004. An easy-to-obtain edition of Addison's influential play.

Adler, Mortimer. *How to Think About Great Ideas: From the Great Books of Western Civilization*. Chicago: Open Court, 2000. A traditional defense of the great books from one of the most influential proponents of the classics.

Ambrose, Stephen. *Undaunted Courage*. New York: Simon and Schuster, 1996. A thrilling and moving account of the expedition of Lewis and Clark by one of America's greatest historians.

Aristophanes. *The Complete Plays*. New York: Bantam, 1962, reprints. The most convenient edition in one volume, but some of the translations could be improved. Ancient comedy is very hard to translate into contemporary idiom.

Aristotle. *Poetics*. Trans. Malcolm Heath. New York: Penguin, 1996. Aristotle's *Poetics* is essential to understanding how the Greeks viewed the tragedies.

Bass, S. Jonathan. *Blessed Are the Peacemakers: Martin Luther King Jr., Eight White Religious Leaders, and the "Letter from a Birmingham Jail."* Baton Rouge: Louisiana State University Press, 2001. A superb study of the historical context of this fundamental work in the freedom of conscience.

Bloom, Harold. *George Orwell*. New York: Chelsea House, 1987. A biography by a leading British intellectual.

Boethius. *On the Consolation of Philosophy*. Trans. V. E. Watts. London, New York: Penguin, 1969. A good, convenient translation.

Boyle, Nicholas. *Goethe: The Poet and the Age*. Oxford: Oxford University Press, 1991. An excellent introduction to the achievement of Goethe.

Brabazon, James. *Albert Schweitzer: A Biography*. Syracuse: Syracuse University Press, 2000. Perhaps the best biography of Schweitzer.

Brown, Raymond. *An Introduction to the Gospel of John*. New York: Doubleday, 2003. A recent, controversial interpretation.

Burckhardt, Jacob. *The Civilization of the Renaissance in Italy*. Trans. S. G. C. Middlemore. New York: Harper, 1958. The brilliant account of Renaissance Italy by the great 19th-century historian of ideas. Fundamental to understanding the audience of Machiavelli's comedy.

Cicero. *On Old Age*. Trans. Frank Copley. Ann Arbor: University of Michigan Press, 1971, reprints. An easy-to-read translation.

Dalby, Andrew. *Rediscovering Homer*. New York: Norton, 2006. A summary of recent views of Homer's epics, which general readers might find instructive.

Denby, David. *Great Books: My Adventures with Homer, Rousseau, Wolff, and Other Indestructible Writers of the Western World*. New York: Simon and Schuster, 1996. An entertaining story of one man's journey with the great books.

D'Este, Carlo. *Patton: A Genius for War*. New York: Harper, 1995. A superb and sympathetic biography.

Dobson, Michael. *The Oxford Companion to Shakespeare*. New York, Oxford: Oxford University Press, 2001. An invaluable work of reference.

Dostoevsky, Fyodor. *The Brothers Karamazov*. Trans. Constance Garnett. New York: Norton, 1976. A standard translation with helpful supplementary material.

Ehrman, Bart. *Misquoting Jesus: The Story Behind Who Changed the Bible and Why*. New York: Harper, 2005. A trendy book, which is stimulating rather than convincing.

Ellis, Jeremy. *His Excellency, George Washington*. New York: Knopf, 2004. An engaging biography of Washington.

Erasmus, Desiderius. *The Praise of Folly*. Trans. Clarence Miller. New Haven: Yale University Press, 1979. A good translation and scholarly edition.

Euripides. *The Complete Greek Tragedies*. Edited by David Grene and Richmond Lattimore. Chicago: University of Chicago Press, 1959. The best translation of all the Greek tragedies, with excellent introductions.

Everitt, Antony. *Cicero: The Life and Times of Rome's Greatest Politician.* New York: Random House, 2001. A recent, popular account.

Fantham, Elaine. *Women in the Classical World.* New York, Oxford: Oxford University Press, 1994. An analysis from a feminist perspective.

Fears, J. Rufus. *The Wisdom of History* (2007), *Books That Have Made History: Books That Can Change Your Life* (2005), *Churchill* (2001), *Famous Greeks* (2001), *Famous Romans* (2001), *A History of Freedom* (2001). Chantilly, VA: The Teaching Company. These lecture courses provide historical background to themes discussed in *Life Lessons from the Great Books.*

Frank, Joseph. *Dostoevsky.* Princeton: Princeton University Press, 1976–2002. An exhaustive four-volume biography.

Goethe, Johann Wolfgang von. *Selected Works.* Trans. Nicholas Boyle. New York: Knopf, 2000. An excellent translation of *Werther.*

Gottfried von Strasburg. *Tristan and Isolde.* Trans. A. T. Hatto. Baltimore: Penguin, 1960. A reliable translation with a good introduction.

———. *Tristan and Isolde.* Trans. J. L. Weston. New York: AMS Press, 1970. A reprint of the translation and a reconstruction of the ending of the story by one of the most brilliant scholars of medieval literature.

Greenblatt, Stephen. *Will in the World: How Shakespeare Became Shakespeare.* New York: Norton, 2004. An engaging, modern attempt to explain the genius of Shakespeare.

Griffin. Miriam. *Nero: The End of a Dynasty.* New Haven: Yale University Press, 1985. A good biography of the emperor Seneca tried to serve.

Gummere, Richard. *Seneca: The Philosopher and His Modern Message.* New York: Cooper Square, 1963. Still the best introduction for the general student.

Hammond, J. R. *An Orwell Companion.* New York: St. Martin's Press, 1982. An indispensable reference work for those really interested in Orwell.

Hanson, Victor. *A War Like No Other: How the Athenians and Spartans Fought the Peloponnesian War*. New York: Random House, 2005. A detailed recent history of the war, drawing lessons for our own day.

Homer. *The Iliad of Homer*. Trans. Richmond Lattimore. Chicago: University of Chicago Press, 1961. A magnificent story in a magnificent translation.

———. *The Odyssey of Homer*. Trans. Richmond Lattimore. New York: Harper, 1967. The immortal story translated by the most brilliant 20th-century translator of the classics.

Huxley, Aldous. *Brave New World*. New York: Harper, 1932, reprints. The chilling vision of a future that is with us now, at least in part.

———. *Brave New World Revisited*. New York: Harper, 1958. An account of Huxley's own intellectual and spiritual journey.

Josephus. *The Jewish War*. Trans. H. St. J. Thackeray. Cambridge: Harvard University Press, 1927, reprints. Still the best translation of this major historical work.

Kraut, Richard. *The Cambridge Companion to Plato*. Cambridge, New York: Cambridge University Press, 1992. An essential work of reference.

Lambdin, Robert. *Encyclopedia of Medieval Literature*. Westport, CT: Greenwood Press, 2000. A valuable reference work.

Lape, Susan. *Reproducing Athens: Menander's Comedy, Democratic Culture, and the Hellenistic City*. Princeton: Princeton University Press, 2004. An interesting example of how contemporary classical scholars approach Greek literature.

Lawrence, T. E. *Seven Pillars of Wisdom*. New York: Anchor, 1991. A reprint of Lawrence's 1926 book. Fascinating but difficult to read because of its discursive style. Lawrence was not satisfied with it.

Lewis, Meriwether, and William Clark. *The Journals of Lewis and Clark*. Edited by Bernard DeVoto. Boston, New York: Houghton Mifflin, 1953, reprints. The best abridgement, with an excellent introduction.

Machiavelli, Niccolò. *The Comedies of Machiavelli*. Trans. David Sices and James Atkinson. Indianapolis: Hackett, 2007. A lively translation, with a helpful introduction.

Maimonides. *The Guide of the Perplexed*. Trans. Shlomo Pines. Chicago: University of Chicago Press, 1979. A medieval, philosophical writing of fundamental importance to understanding the thought of modern Judaism.

Marenbon, John. *Boethius*. Oxford, New York: Oxford University Press, 2003. An excellent, recent biography.

McConica, James. *Erasmus*. New York, Oxford: Oxford University Press, 1991. A useful biography.

Menander. *Plays and Fragments*. Trans. N. P. Miller. New York: Penguin, 1987. The best edition for the general reader.

More, Thomas. *Utopia*. Trans. George Logan, Robert Adams, and Clarence Miller. Cambridge: Cambridge University Press, 1995. A superb scholarly edition and translation.

Morford, Mark, and Robert Lenardon. *Classical Mythology*. New York, Oxford: Oxford University Press, 1999. A good, well-illustrated textbook.

Murray, Gilbert. *Euripides and His Age*. New York, Oxford: Oxford University Press, 1965. A reprint of what is still the best introduction to Euripides for the general reader, by a modern Humanist.

The Nibelungenlied: Prose Translation. Trans. A. T. Hatto. New York: Penguin, 1965. A good translation with a helpful and detailed introduction.

Oates, Stephen. *With Malice Toward None: The Life of Abraham Lincoln*. New York: New American Library, 1997. The best one-volume biography.

Orwell, George. *Animal Farm*. New York: Signet, 1946. Orwell's satirical novel of the failure of revolutions.

Patton, George. *War As I Knew It*. New York: Bantam, 1980. A posthumous book based on Patton's diaries.

Plato. *Timaeus, Critias, Cleitophon, Menexenus, Epistles*. Trans. R. G. Bury. Cambridge: Harvard University Press, 1929, reprints. The best translation, with a helpful historical introduction.

Plutarch. *Lives of the Noble Grecians and Romans*. Trans. John Dryden. New York: Modern Library, 2000. This new edition of a classic translation gives the reader a better understanding of the whole of Plutarch's work and its moral purpose than do other modern translations that break his biographies down into artificial units.

Roosevelt, Theodore. *The Works of Theodore Roosevelt*. New York: Charles Scribner's Sons, 1926. A 20-volume collection of the president's writings, including *An Autobiography* and *American Ideals*.

Schweitzer, Albert. *Out of My Life and Thought*. New York: Holt, 1949. Schweitzer's account of his spiritual journey.

————. *Reverence for Life*. New York: Harper and Row, 1969. A more detailed discussion of Schweitzer's philosophy of life.

Seneca. *Letters and Dialogues*. Trans. C. D. N. Costa. New York: Penguin, 1997. A convenient edition.

————. *Moral Essays*. Trans. John Basore. Cambridge: Harvard University Press, 1928, reprints. Still the best translation.

Shakespeare, William. *The Complete Plays and Poems of William Shakespeare*. Edited by William Allan Neilson and Charles Jarvis Hill. New York: Houghton Mifflin, 1942, reprints. The best complete edition, especially useful for its introductions and notes, which, unlike many more recent editions, allow Shakespeare to speak for himself.

Singer, Isaac Bashevis. *The Penitent*. New York: Ballantine, 1983. The powerful novel of a spiritual journey.

Smallwood, Mary. *The Jews under Roman Rule*. Leiden: Brill, 1976. A detailed, scholarly study; the best in its field.

The Song of Roland. Trans. Dorothy Sayers. Baltimore: Penguin, 1957. A fluid translation with an excellent introduction by a woman who was both a good medievalist and a mystery writer.

Sophocles. *The Complete Greek Tragedies*. Edited by David Grene and Richmond Lattimore. Chicago: Chicago University Press, 1957, reprints. By far, the best translations of the Greek tragedies.

Spalding, Matthew, and Patrick Garrity. *A Sacred Union of Citizens: George Washington's Farewell Address and the American Character*. New York: Rowman and Littlefield, 1996. A superb edition of Washington's *Address*, with an insightful discussion.

Whitman, Cedric. *Sophocles: A Study of Heroic Humanism*. Cambridge: Harvard University Press, 1966. An interpretative study by a Humanist of learning and insight.

Wiesel, Elie. *All Rivers Run to the Sea: Memoirs*. New York: Knopf, 1995. This autobiography is fundamental to understanding the man and his achievement.

————. *Night*. New York: Hill and Wang, 2006. A recent edition of this powerful novel.

Wigoder, Geoffrey. *The New Encyclopedia of Judaism*. New York: New York University Press, 2002. A helpful work of reference.

Wilson, Jeremy. *Lawrence of Arabia*. New York: Atheneum, 1990. The most detailed biography but one written without a full appreciation of Lawrence as a military genius.

Notes